Four-Block Quilts

Echoes of History,
Pieced Boldly & Appliquéd Freely

By Terry Clothier Thompson

Four-Block Quilts
Echoes of History: Pieced Boldly and Appliquéd Freely

By Terry Clothier Thompson

Edited by Deb Rowden

Book and cover design by Kelly Ludwig, Ludwig Design

Photography by Bill Krzyzanowski

Production assistance by Jo Ann Groves

Drawings: L. Eric Craven

Templates by Gary Embrey

Published by Kansas City Star Books

1729 Grand Blvd., Kansas City, Missouri 64108

Copyright © 2004 by The Kansas City Star Co.

First Edition, first printing

ISBN: 0-9746012-6-8

Printed in the United States of America by Walsworth Publishing Co.

To order copies, call StarInfo, (816-234-4636) and say "Books."

✶ KANSAS CITY STAR BOOKS

The Quilter's Home Page

www.PickleDish.com

Four-Block Quilts

Echoes of History,
Pieced Boldly & Appliquéd Freely

By Terry Clothier Thompson

Dedicated to my loving mother
Esther Cline Richardson

With thanks and gratitude to the following people for contributing to the success of this beautiful book

Historical references

Grant Clothier

Artishia Dotten and Mary Estelle Williams

Nancy Hornback

Betty Kinnamon and Vida Clothier

Nancy Maes-Simonetti

Shirley Jean Moss

Billie Lee Snyder Thornburg and
  Bertie Snyder Elfeldt, daughters of
  Grace Snyder, for books and
  information

Kansas State Historical Society, Nancy
  Sherbert, curator of manuscripts

Terri Raburn,
  Nebraska State Historical Society

Pat Walters, Republic County
  Historical Society Museum

Riley County Historical Society

Mary Brennan, Shiloh Museum,
  Springdale, Arkansas

Rhonda Wetjen, University of Iowa Press

Appliquers, Piecers, Quilters and Binders

Jean Stanclift

Pam Mayfield

Karalee Fisher

Rosie Mayhew

Lori Kukuk

Esther Richardson

Ann Thomas

Vital help

Cherié Ralston

Shannon Richards

Kent Richards

Kate Rowden

Betsy Rowden

Susan Russell, for sharing the story of her
  grandmother Neva Banks' exhortation
to "Piece boldly".

Cindy Schott

Kathy Schott Gates

About the author

During the twentieth century . . . it may be argued that Kansas women have done more than follow others: They have led the way and developed trends that have created various national styles . . . .

Carrie Hall, Rose Kretsinger, Scioto Imhoff Danner and Terry Thompson are a few of those whose patterns have achieved national circulation, giving the state its well-deserved reputation as 'quilt country.'

----Kansas Quilts and Quilters, University Press of Kansas, 1993

Terry Clothier Thompson has been on the forefront of our current quilt revival.

Born into the fifth generation of a Kansas pioneer family, she grew up in the Wichita area. She watched her grandmother sew and quilt during visits to the family farm west of Hutchinson called Peace Creek.

Her stitching passion began when she sewed calico dresses for her daughter. With the leftover scraps, she made a quilt. She became passionate.

Her family's move to Kansas City brought the opportunity to teach patchwork classes at Johnson County Community College. In 1973, she opened "The Quilting Bee," an anomaly at that time: a store devoted totally to quilting. The shop was located on the Country Club Plaza until 1984. She designed a unique line of patterns that she still sells nationwide. Another career highlight was her selection to represent quiltmakers in the Kansas-Bloomingdales' promotion of Kansas products in 1988. She was a principal documenter for the Kansas Quilt Project from 1986 to 1989 and a co-author of Kansas Quilts and Quilters, published in 1993 by the University Press of Kansas.

In addition to her appliqué patterns, Terry has written six books, each a collection of family stories in different eras, with quilts designed to go along with the stories.

Her passion for quiltmaking is contagious. She has an extensive collection of vintage fabrics, quilts, lace, and all kinds of needlework. She also designs a line of reproduction fabrics for Moda with Barbara Brackman. For more information about Terry, check out her web site: terrythompson.com.

She raised two children and enjoys her four wonderful grandchildren.

1

Foreword
Four-Block Quilts

Future quilt historians will look back at the turn of this century as one of the golden ages of appliqué. Today's quiltmakers are creating quilts equal to the appliquéd masterpieces of the 1850's and the 1930's.

Our interest in appliqué grows out of a certain sophistication. Quilters who acquired excellent needlework skills in years of piecing quilts are now looking for new challenges. Designers who have explored the infinite complexities of the triangle and the square are working with more naturalistic shapes. Artists trying to capture nature's beauty are inspired by today's fabrics rather than paint. As a quilt historian I am always looking for the influences that trigger trends, the individuals who inspire, the patterns that are practical, the prizewinners that create copies.

In the January, 1994 issue of Cover Stories, the newsletter of the Canadian Quilt Study Group, Maureen McGee wrote a query to the "Members Want to Know" column.

"I'm seeing quite a revival here (Kansas) in four block quilts—those big, 30" or so, appliquéd blocks that were popular in the 1800's. Do you see much of that in your area? I suspect quilting trends vary a lot from region to region, depending who the local teachers or trendsetters are." [1]

I never found the time to answer Maureen's query with my thoughts on the topic, so I'm glad to respond here in the introduction to Terry's book.

Indeed trends do vary a lot from region to region, and after studying the magnificent appliqué quilts made in Emporia, Kansas, in the 1930's, I agree that local teachers and trendsetters are the significant factor. In Emporia, the individual was Rose Good Kretsinger, whom I described as possessing the qualities that make a trendsetter. She was innovative, a model; she generated novel ideas and established high standards. To quote myself:

"The innovative individual must be competitive, but it is more important that she or he be cooperative. She must be willing to share her ideas through formal training or informal methods, such as the hand-drawn patterns and one-to-one assistance that Rose Kretsinger offered."[2]

Maureen's observation of a recent trend in Kansas is perceptive. I believe that Terry Thompson is behind this trend. Terry has been teaching her Applique by the Yard classes in Kansas and Missouri for several years. Her revival of the four-block quilt is innovative; she is an effective teacher and her practical patterns and advice make it easy to produce these striking quilts.

With the publication of this book, quiltmakers from Florida to Canada will have the opportunity to learn from Terry. I expect to see her influence extend far beyond her home state.

Barbara Brackman
January, 2004
Lawrence, Kansas

1. Letter from Maureen McGee in Cover Stories: Newsletter of the Canadian Quilt Study Group, Volume 5, Number 3, January 1994, pg. 5.
2. Barbara Brackman, "Emporia 1925-1950: Reflections on a Community," in Kansas Quilts and Quilters, (Lawrence, Kansas: University Press of Kansas, 1994) 124.

3

Four-Block Quilts
Echoes of History: Pieced Boldly and Appliquéd Freely

Day of appliqué participants: Nancy Maes-Simonettii, Eleanor Malone, Beverly Hewitt, Virginia Moody, Florence Reiter, Sharon Allen, Zelma Lee, Mary Blackburn, Barbara Cooper, Martha Houston, Winnie Laughlin, Norma Johnston, Nancy Hornback, Doris Callaway, Irma Hall, Irlene Withroder, Bernita Lawrence, Ann Taylor and Terry Thompson.

The virtues of working big

How you can lose your fear of appliqué with Four-Block Quilts

I've always loved appliqué. And I've worked for years to get quilters past their fear of it.

In 1987, while documenting quilts in Greensburg, Kansas, for the Kansas Quilt Project, I realized at the end of the day that I had seen 23 four block quilts. All were 19th century red and green appliquéd quilts. As a former quilt dealer, I bought and sold many quilts, but I paid no real attention to the four-block pieced and appliquéd quilts that briefly passed through my hands. The quilts in Greensburg got my attention.

I wondered what was so appealing about making four very large 36-inch blocks. I decided to invite 17 quilting friends to my farm in Peace Creek, Kansas, for a day of appliqué. The only conditions were that they know how to appliqué and that they like it. I wanted no whining.

We all gathered in my living room and I gave each woman a kit to make one block. We spread the blocks out on the floors, the beds, and countertops because we were working with really big blocks, not the usual 12-inch block that could be worked on by six or so women around one table. By the end of the day, we had our appliqué pieces cut out and basted onto the blocks. We agreed to continue work on the blocks during the summer, between gardening and caring for children, then to meet again in the fall. My friends all returned with their finished blocks and their thoughts about the virtues of working BIG.

Their comments varied, and most were positive about their sewing experience that summer. Here are some of their observations:

"By gathering the block up in my hands, I actually had something to hold on to as I appliquéd around each pattern piece. This helped the arthritis in my hands."

"Pre-basting the seam allowance under each piece before I basted it to the block helped me appliqué so quickly, it was worth the little extra time it took to prepare it first. Long gentle curves allow uninterrupted sewing rhythm."

"Appliqué is so forgiving. The appliqués can be cut without regard to grain. Appliqué is on the bias works so smoothly."

I spent that summer collecting quilts, looking through my books for designs for 36-inch blocks. I saw fewer pieced blocks and realized almost any quilt block can be enlarged to the 30-to 36-inch format. Not every block measured exactly 36", but most reached the 30-to 32-inch range. Electric Quilt 5 software was a great help in drafting the pieced blocks in this book.

My quilting life totally changed that summer of 1987. I knew I had found my niche in appliqué. My hands just would not work "small" or intricate anymore. I loved the large designs and the big blocks. I began teaching about four-block quilts and called my patterns "Appliqué Pieced by the Yard."

HAVE NO FEAR!

Now that you know how I came to the concept of four-block quilts, let's examine something I call the F.O.A. (Fear of Appliqué).

In 32 years of teaching, I have often heard: "I love the look of hand appliqué but I hate the process." When I taught myself to appliqué, the only book available about it was Jean Ray Laury's "Appliqué Stitchery," published in 1966. She

6

advocated using the top running stitch and my first attempts with appliqué seemed so easy and carefree. I taught hand appliqué using the running stitch for several years. But in the 1980's I switched to teaching the blind stitch technique for hand appliqué. It was probably because of the growing interest in Baltimore Album quilts.

I believe we lost scores of appliquérs because the blind stitch is so hard for beginning appliquérs to master. They had too many failures and too few successes and gave up.

But here's the good news. You can return to master the pleasures of appliqué by choosing a four-block pattern and using the top running stitch.

Let's go one step further and look at the toughest challenge for beginning appliquérs. It is eye-hand coordination.

I appliqué in a clockwise direction so I can see the turned-under seam allowance. If I sew counter-clockwise, I cannot see over the top of the fold. It seems awkward to me. It's not wrong, but it's wrong for me. I know many experienced teachers and artists who sew counter-clockwise — it works for them. But if you are uncomfortable with appliqué and maybe your shoulder aches or your arm tires easily, consider changing the direction that you sew. It might make a big difference for you. After I teach this method, at least two or three people come up after class and tell me, "It works. I feel better, I sew faster and I love to appliqué now."

I sew in a comfortable chair, with good light and a bed pillow on my lap to rest my hands and arms on. I then sew in a natural direction, with my arm coming toward my body, constantly turning the block as I sew, and not stretching my arm and hand in an awkward motion, which pulls the shoulder muscles. Try stitching clockwise and counter-clockwise to see which works best for you.

After you are comfortable with the top running stitch, which is perfect for these folk art blocks, you can move on to the blind stitch if you like.

The top running stitch (by hand or machine) flattens the folded edge of the appliqué. If sewn on printed fabric with matching thread, it is not even seen. If you want an embellished look, sew in a contrasting color that will show. I use the contrasting running stitch on my cowboy quilts to look like the leather stitches on saddles and tack.

The virtues of the blind stitch are that the stitches are hidden and will raise the edge of the appliqué so that you have a lovely rounded edge that looks great for more formal appliqué, such as Baltimore quilts or intricate floral designs.

Good appliqué takes practice and patience, and the rewards are ten-fold in relaxation and stress relief.

For everyone who enjoys machine appliqué, you can get a hand-made look using the machine appliqué directions in the "Good Advice" section at that back of this book. Piecers who want the challenge of piecing a four-block quilt will enjoy the process too.

THE HISTORY IN THIS BOOK

When I was little, I often had a dream that I was sleeping under a covered wagon, looking up into the great big sky. I've always been drawn to the 19th century. I was spellbound by the stories of the women in my family, how they braved life on the prairie. I've continued gathering stories — from diaries, books, and letters — throughout my life. I have such admiration for pioneer women and how brave they were.

Maybe that's why the stories that follow have resonated with me: brave Bess Corey, industrious Mary Sears. I've studied Grace Snyder's inspiring life since meeting her years ago. Some of these women documented their lives in letters, some through stories they told to their families. Others left only their quilts behind — Bird Russ's and Mary Scruggs's lives remain tantalizing mysteries. Some stories have come from my students, who have shared ancestor's letters.

I've always wanted to combine four-block quilts with the stories of pioneer women. They fit together. Pioneer women worked so hard. Once their life was established on the frontier, they had free moments to make quilts again. These quilts they inspired seem like ones they would have worked on. They were achievable.

We also offer projects these women might have made. They are practical items they would have lived with and worn — even things to occupy their children.

Today's women can relate to that. They, too, need an escape, but one that doesn't take too much time out of their busy lives.

The quilts and projects inspired by these women offer something for everyone who loves to sew. They are fast and easy to make - in a matter of weeks, not years.

Enjoy the journey.

Mary Sears

Mary A. Sears
(Latest photograph taken at Chillicothe, Ohio, February, 1917.)

"Go West and Grow Up with the Country"

Mary Sears, Settler

Mary Sears lived the early history of the Sunflower State.

As a young bride in the mid-1850s, Mary Sears heard renowned journalist Horace Greeley speak at a dinner in the Hudson River Valley. His advice to "Go West, young man, and grow up with the country" became her young family's destiny, as she, husband Charles, and baby Emma headed west in 1856.

After a few years in Iowa, the Sears started for California in June, 1859, with Emma and 15-month-old son William. William frightened his family when he wandered away from the wagon and disappeared into the tall prairie grass. For the rest of the journey, a clothesline was fastened around his waist, with the other end tied to the wagon when he wanted to wander.

The Sears stopped in Lecompton, Kansas, to see an old friend on the fourth of July. Tired of traveling, they claimed 160 acres southeast of Lawrence, built a log cabin, and stayed. Mary was in Kansas six weeks before she saw a white woman. Indians passed their cabin frequently.

PIONEERING
IN
KANSAS

IOWA TO KANSAS IN AN OX WAGON

EXPERIENCES
OF
CAPT. CHARLES M. SEARS AND FAMILY
IN THE '50s

BY L. WILLIAM THAVIS
WASHINGTON NEWSPAPER CORRESPONDENT

Drought that year sent many settlers back East, but the Sears moved to Lawrence, where Charles cut grass in Bismarck Grove, north of the Kansas River, to sustain his family. He then taught school, after walking 14 miles to Baldwin City to get his teaching certificate. He built the first schoolhouse in the community of Hesper, where people gathered for literary, religious, and social activities.

Mary's activities included being a member of the Hesper Lyceum, a literary society, sewing and quilting parties, all-day visits with neighbors, trips to hear orators, and evening parties of dancing and game-playing.

Mary's family were living on their farm in 1863 when Quantrill's raiders attacked Lawrence. Mary's husband, Charles, was a captain with the Kansas State Militia (this troop was known locally as the Hesper Company, named for the village where they met for drill). The militia pursued the Missouri mob as they headed home after attacking Lawrence. Charles was wounded in the pursuit. Mary called that the "most tragic and dramatic experience of my pioneer days in Kansas."

The Sears were in Kansas for the infamous grasshopper invasion of 1875-76. Mary once found her house and cellar full of them "so thick that you could not step or put your finger down without touching them."

Mary lived in Kansas for 25 years. Her husband served one term as a state legislator, three terms as justice of the peace, one term as county commissioner, and in the 17th Kansas Infantry during the Civil War. The family moved to Ohio in 1882.

Mary Sears, Mount Lebanon, NY, 1854

MRS. CHARLES M. SEARS
(From daguerreotype taken at Mount
Lebanon, N. Y., 1854.)

"Preparedness at that time was our watchword. Mr. Sears prepared the wagon in which we were to live and make our journey, and I made ready my trousseau - by hand at that. While we were preparing to leave we learned that five other families were planning to make the same trip; a conference was arranged, and it was decided that all would start together. All the ladies agreed to make and wear bloomers instead of skirts. I joined them in this plan and we found them very comfortable and convenient for climbing in and out of the wagons and working about our camps. We never regretted our change in costume."

"But for that (their journey west) we were well prepared with a Dutch oven, in which I baked my bread, and a tin reflector which we stood before the fire and before which I baked my new-made pies and cakes. They were just as good as any I had made in a nice, convenient kitchen. This was proven by the appetites of those who ate them."

" We made no mistake in taking the cows for they supplied us with milk and butter. I did not have to churn, for we put the milk in an old-fashioned dash churn in the rear end of the wagon and the jolting over the rough road churned the milk into butter, which I soon prepared when we stopped to camp."

On arriving in Kansas: " The first words he said to me were: "Why, where is your complexion?" I answered: "Oh, I left that on the way.""

When spring came it brought rain, and we moved back to the farm. It has been said that "every bitter has its sweet." The expanding prairies were dry, but they were like a garden of flowers - beautiful pink phlox, the pink and white wild peas, the beautiful wild rose and the dainty sensitive plants, which closed at the gentlest touch; these the little ones delighted to gather and they brought them to me in lovely bouquets.

"I never regretted that I became a charter member of the Hesper Lyceum. This was one of the joys that came to me in the West. Even though the road was long and dreary and we were sometimes weary, our faithful team, "Buck" and "Broad," always carried us safely there and

The Sears homestead as it appeared in 1890. It was destroyed by fire in 1916.

THE OLD HOMESTEAD

back with our precious load of little ones; for we always took our children along with us, with comforts and buffalo robes to keep them warm. I derived much benefit from the association I formed at this society, for they gave me new courage to bear up and go bravely on."

"The day of the pioneer is past. No such opportunity will again come in this country as came to me, to travel hundreds of miles with oxen teams and settle in a frontier wilderness, where on all sides could be heard the howl of the wolves and often be seen the deer and antelopes bounding across the hills, while only 30 miles away ranged the great buffaloes that provided us always with our winter meat."

--Mary's life experiences are documented in the pamphlet "Pioneering in Kansas: Experiences of Capt. Charles M. Sears and Family in the `50s" by L. William Thavis.

Mary's son W. H. Sears read this paper at the Kansas State Society annual banquet on Kansas Day, January 29, 1917. His mother was then 81 years old and read the same paper, entitled "Pioneer Traveling", to the Century Club in Chillicothe, Ohio.

Mary's son William drew this sketch of the family homestead in 1859 from memory. Looking northwest toward Lawrence, it shows Bald Mount on the left, Blue Mount in the center and Mount Oread on the right. Illustrations in this chapter courtesy Kansas State Historical Society.

Mary Sears "Sunflowers"

"The expanding prairies...were like a garden of flowers"

74" x 74"

These sunflower designs are from an appliquéd quilt made by Mary Brown (1777-1861) in Cecil County, Maryland. I have always admired the pattern and have adapted it to fit the four-block format. I chose the traditional colors of the original quilt—red, yellow/gold and green. You may choose any color combination that pleases you.

15

The Sunflower quilt seems a good illustration of Mary Sears' pioneer story. Imagine her suntanned face when she first saw a field of blooming Kansas sunflowers nearly 150 years ago.

The small project is a 19th century roll-up sewing case. Women kept needles, thimbles, thread, pins and scissors for safekeeping in this useful sewing kit. It fit nicely in a ladies pocket for travel. Young Civil War soldiers used a roll-up as a sewing repair kit for replacing buttons on uniforms, mending tears in their clothing and as a safe place to tuck a lock of a loved one's hair.

Please read all directions before beginning.

Yardage

Baskets

- ¼ yard stripe or floral for 4 baskets

Background and Borders

- 3 ⅛ yards of soft yellow/gold check for (4) 28 ½" background blocks
- 2 yards of a soft yellow/gold print for borders

Blocks

Greens

- 1 yd. of green for large caylxs, leaves, stems
- ⅛ yd. each of three more greens for leaves, small and medium calyx and stems
- 1 yd. of green for bias vines for borders

Reds

- 1 ½ yard for large and smaller buds
- ¼ yd. for flat piping between blocks (9) 1" strips

Yellow-gold

- 1 yard for large and smaller buds

Choose greens, reds and yellows that contrast with the background blocks. These are traditional colors. You may choose any color combination that pleases you.

Cutting Directions

Follow directions for machine or hand appliqué in Good Advice section at back of book . Note: turn asymetical templates over if you want the image seen in quilt.

- Background blocks: Cut four 28 ½" squares (¼" seam allowance included).

Sunflowers

- Cut (8) red large sunflower B, (8) green large front and back calyx C and A.
- Repeat above for large yellow sunflowers and calyx.

Large Bud E and small bud H

- Cut 15 large E and D and 10 small H and G red buds.
- Cut 8 large D and E and 4 small H and G yellow buds
- Use calyx F for backs of some buds—large or small—or omit from some.

Large, medium and small stems M and L

- Tape full-size stem pieces M together and cut 4 green (one for each block).
- Cut 8 medium stems, reversing some for diversity. The medium stem is created by cutting off the long stem M at the solid line on the stem.
- Cut 29 small stems L, reversing several for diversity.

Large and small leaves

- Cut 28 large leaves K.
- Cut 18 small leaves J.

Sewing Directions

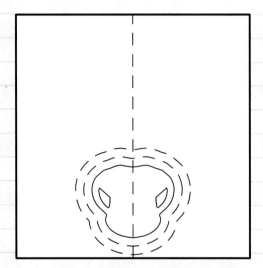

- Follow Good Advice for creating the sunflower leaves, bud and calyx units.
- Fold block in half and press a guideline down the center. Place basket I on center fold 1 ½" from bottom edge.
- Lay out all stems, buds and leaves. Blocks do not have to look identical. Reverse some stems to make it look more natural.
- Pin all units in place. Place on design wall and if everything looks good, baste all pieces. Appliqué in place.
- When all blocks are appliquéd, follow the flat piping instructions in Good Advice. Refer to figure 2 for placement:

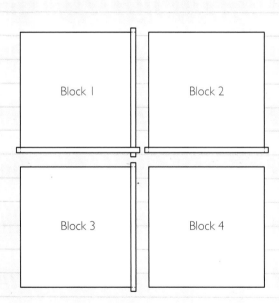

- Block #1 has flat piping on the right side and on the bottom side. Sew one side, then sew bottom piping on letting strips cross over each other at corner. Block #2 has flat piping only on the bottom. Block #3 has piping only on the right side and Block #4 has none.
- After piping is in place, assemble the four blocks as usual. Sew flat piping around entire edge of assembled blocks, as you would binding.

Borders

I admire our foremothers approach to borders on their quilts. Some diligently measured and made border vines meet and curve perfectly at the corners. But many more did not worry about or even attempt to make curves meet in the corners-- they simply ran the vines right off the edge. I designed "Sunflowers" borders to show these uncomplicated borders and make life easier for all.

- Cut top and bottom borders 9 ½" x 56 ½".
- Cut side borders 9 ½" x 74 ½".
- To mark the borders for the vine, fold border in half and press down the center of the border. This is your guide for placing the bias vine.
- You may use the Vine Line tool© I designed for marking borders or make a template of the curve pattern provided.
- Beginning at the left end of the border, place the straight edge of curve template on the pressed center line. Draw with a pencil around the curve. Flip the template over. Line up the straight edge again with the pressed center line and continue your curve. Repeat to the edge of the border. Don't worry about the vine ending up perfectly there. This gives your quilt a 19th century look.
- After borders are marked, make a bias cut vine (see Good Advice at back of book.)
- Lay bias over marked line. Pin in place.
- Arrange bud stems and leaves along vine using picture as a guide. Pin and baste all appliqués and vine for sewing.
- Appliqué all pieces.
- Sew finished borders to quilt center.
- Lori Kukuk machine quilted the blocks with echoes. Follow the shape of the appliqué and repeat about ¼" or more from last line.
- Bind edges.

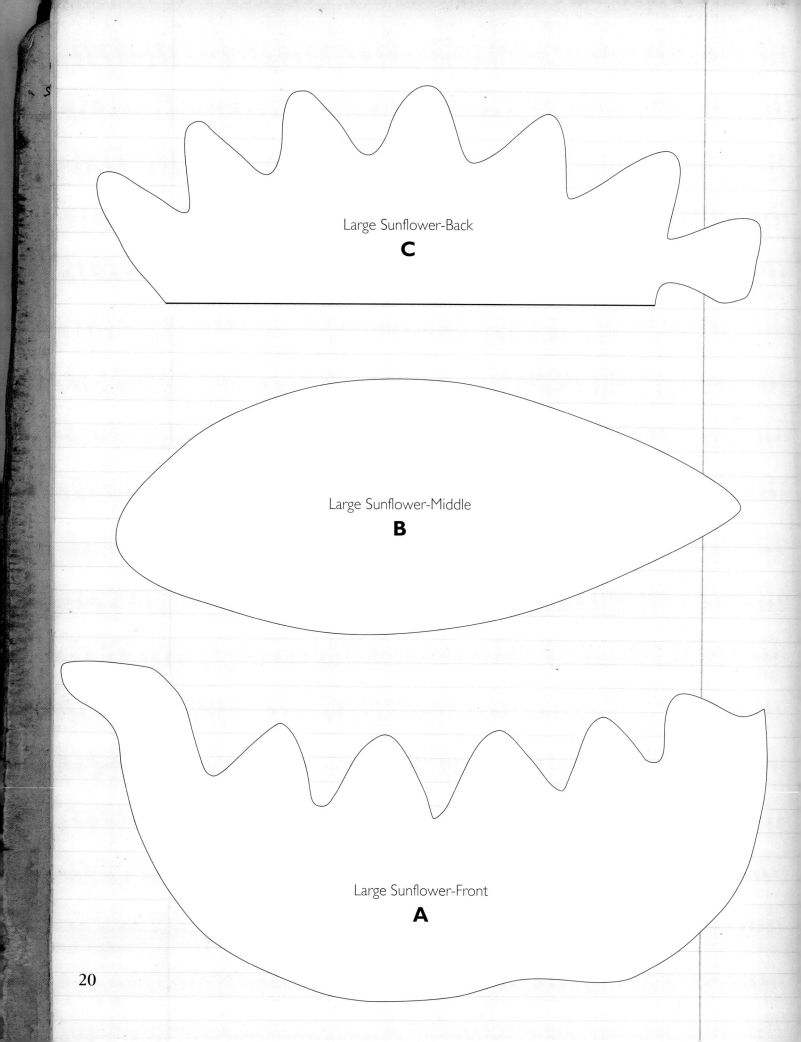

Large Sunflower-Back

C

Large Sunflower-Middle

B

Large Sunflower-Front

A

20

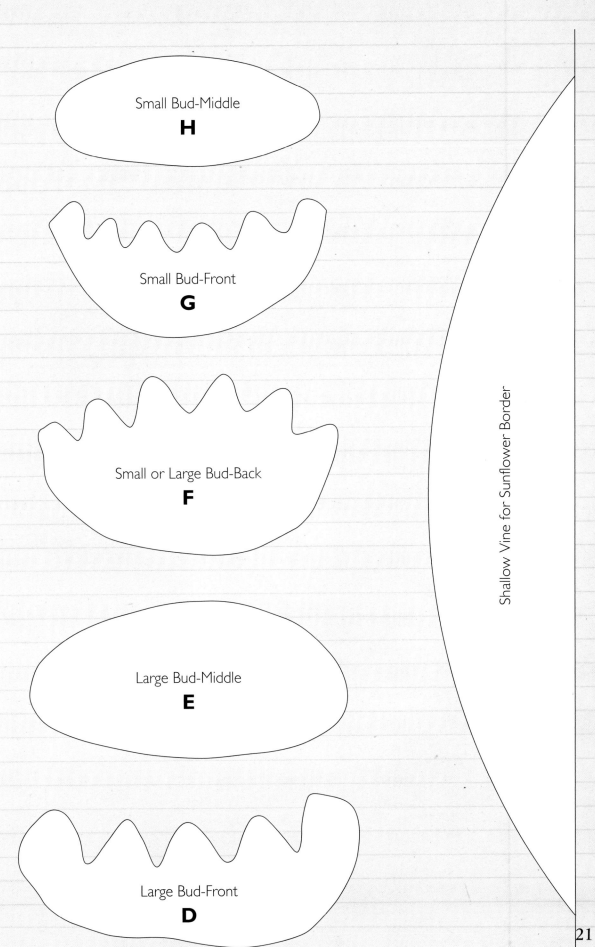

Small Bud-Middle
H

Small Bud-Front
G

Small or Large Bud-Back
F

Large Bud-Middle
E

Large Bud-Front
D

Shallow Vine for Sunflower Border

21

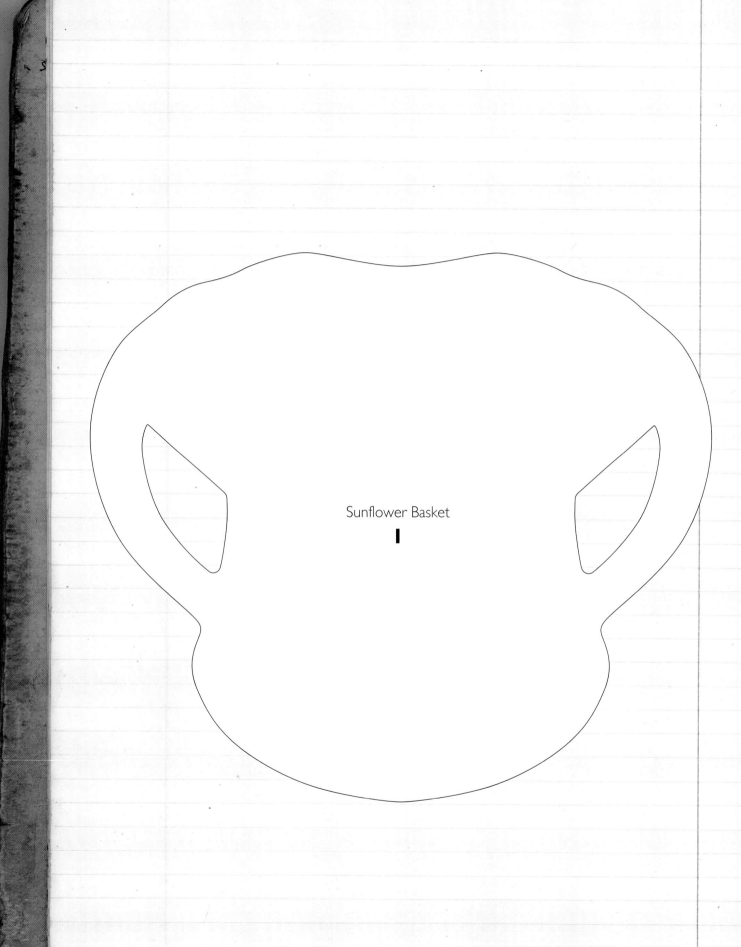

Sunflower Basket

I

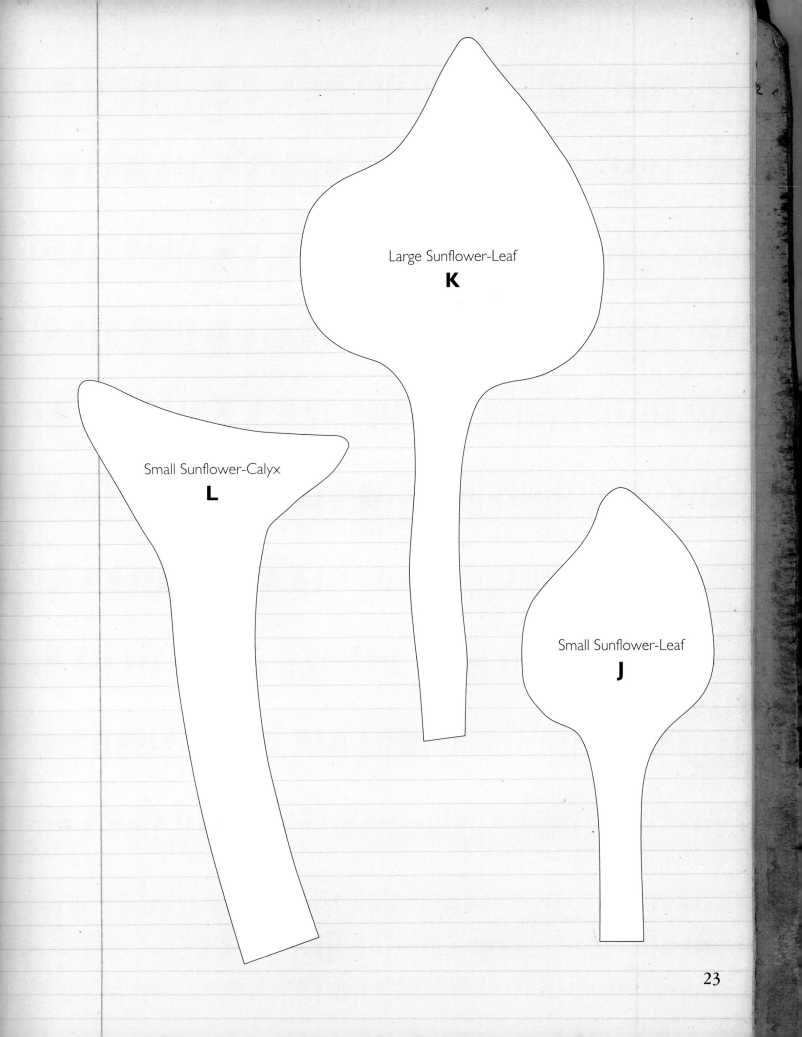

Large Sunflower-Leaf
K

Small Sunflower-Calyx
L

Small Sunflower-Leaf
J

23

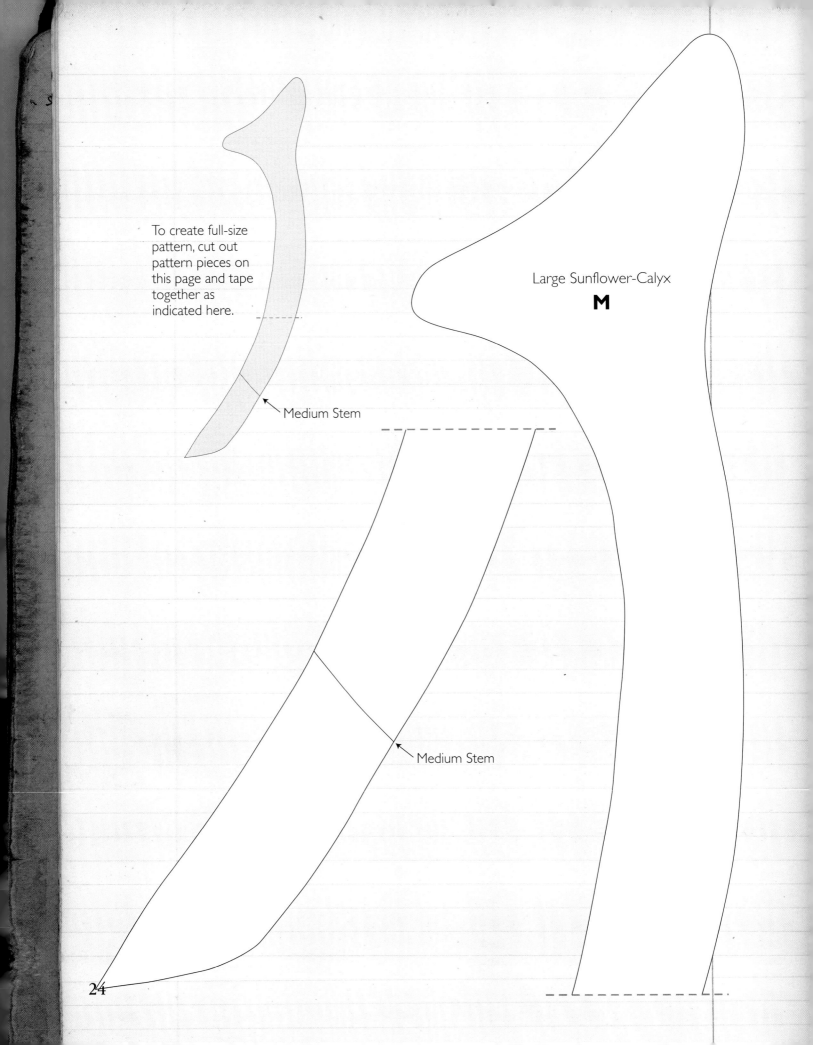

To create full-size pattern, cut out pattern pieces on this page and tape together as indicated here.

Medium Stem

Large Sunflower-Calyx

M

Medium Stem

24

Sewing Case "Huswif"
"Huswif" is German for housewife

Stitch ¼" seams throughout.

Read all directions before beginning this project.

Yardage

- ¼ yard pink, ¼ yard indigo blue for flying geese
- 1 fat quarter of indigo blue for binding (2" x 60")
- Shaded French ribbon – 2 strips, 15" long
- 5" x 7" scraps of (5) prints for (5) pockets and one 8 ½" x 10 ½" print for gathered pocket

Cut

- Cut 2 flaps A of same pink fabric.
- With wrong sides together, sew the two flaps A together all the way around flap. (Fig. 1)
- Cut and piece 7 flying geese blocks. Set blocks as shown in picture—about 21" long. (Fig. 2)

- Sew lined flap to the top of flying geese strip.
- For pockets, double turn 1/4" hem and sew top of each pocket to finish raw edge. (Fig. 3)

- Lay out top pocket with the right side against the wrong side of bottom of the top goose block.
- Sew pocket to goose.
- Repeat for the next four pockets. (Fig. 4)

- Fold pockets back over seams, press, and pin to sides of "A", overlapping the previous pocket. (Fig. 5)

- Turn under ¼" on top edge of fabric for gathered pocket, press.
- Turn under 1" and sew top edge, making a casing for the ribbon ties.
- Cut a slit in the middle of casing for ribbon. Finish edges with a buttonhole stitch. (Fig. 6)

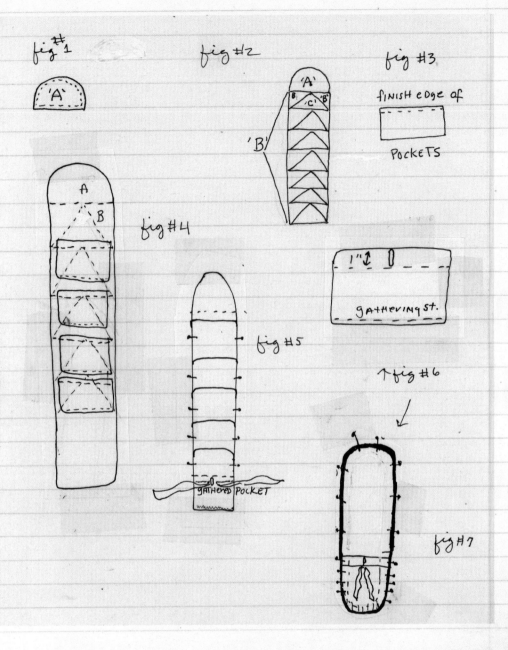

fig #1

fig #2

fig #3

fig #4

fig #5

fig #6

fig #7

'A'

'A'

'B' 'C' 'B'

'B'

A

B

finish edge of

Pockets

1"

gathering st.

gathered pocket

- Run a gathering stitch on bottom of pocket, and gather bottom edge of pocket. Sew to bottom of pocket, wrong sides together.
- Thread ribbon thru slit and pin edges of ribbon to sides of pocket.

- Fold 2" bias binding in half. Pin raw edges of binding to raw edge of Huswif. Sew binding around entire shape. Turn over raw edge and appliqué down. (Fig. 7)

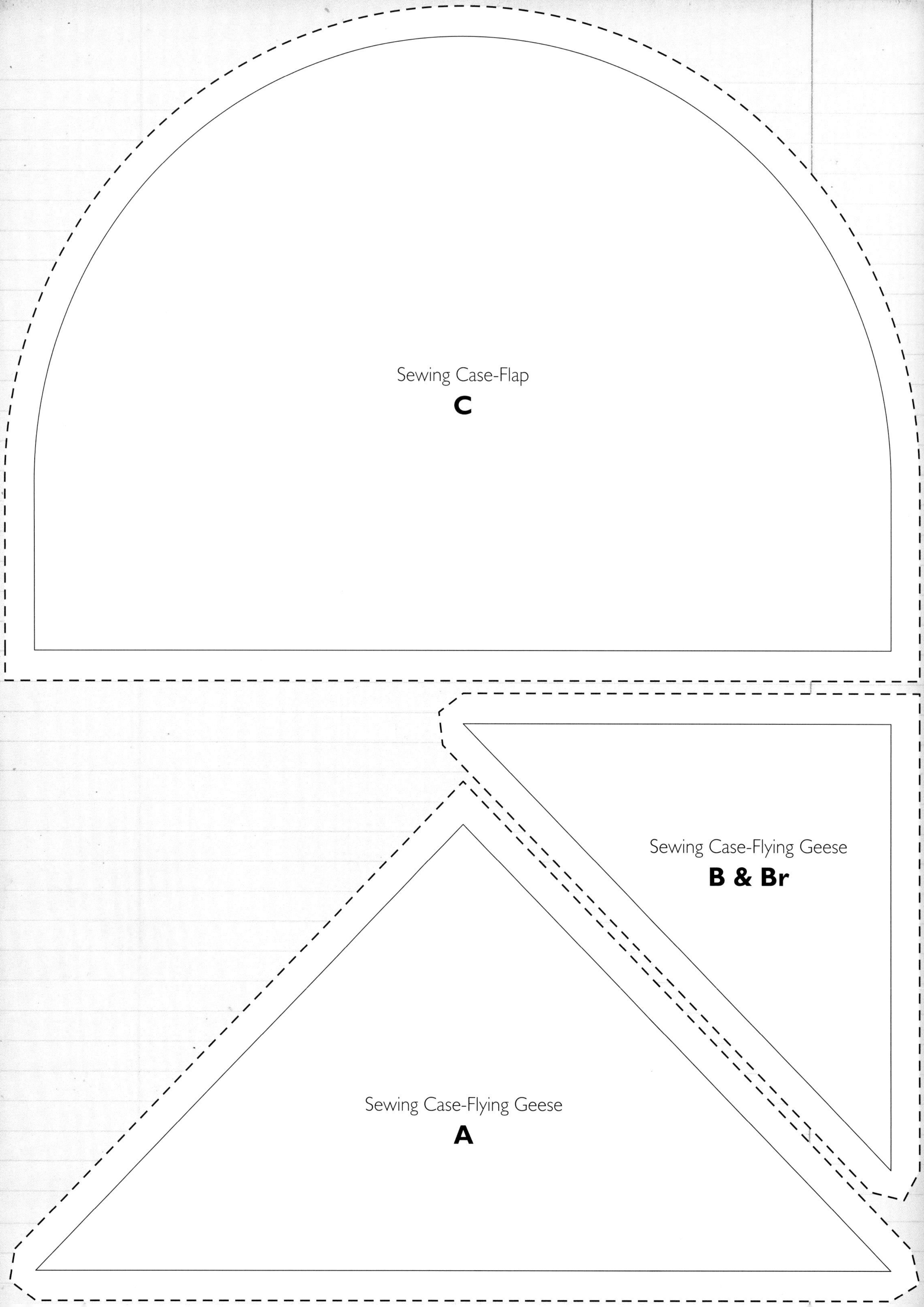

Sewing Case-Flap

C

Sewing Case-Flying Geese

B & Br

Sewing Case-Flying Geese

A

Wool Sunflower Pincushion

Supplies

- 7 ½" square of green wool felt for leaves A
- 7" square of gold wool felt for petals C
- 4 ½" square of brown wool for center B
- Two 9 ½" squares of black wool for stuffed pincushion
- Wool roving or pillow stuffing
- Freezer paper

Sewing

- Cut out templates for all three pattern pieces.
- Press freezer paper templates on back of green and gold felt squares. Cut wool right along the freezer paper edge. No seam allowance is needed. Repeat for circle center.
- Appliqué circle to gold petals by hand or machine, then appliqué petals to green leaves as shown in picture.
- Appliqué finished sunflower to 9 ½" square.
- With right sides together, sew to the other 9 ½" square leaving an opening for turning.
- Turn out the pincushion corners.
- Stuff firmly. Stitch opening closed.

White or clear beads would look like drops of dew on the petals. I placed vintage glass headed pins on my green leaves.

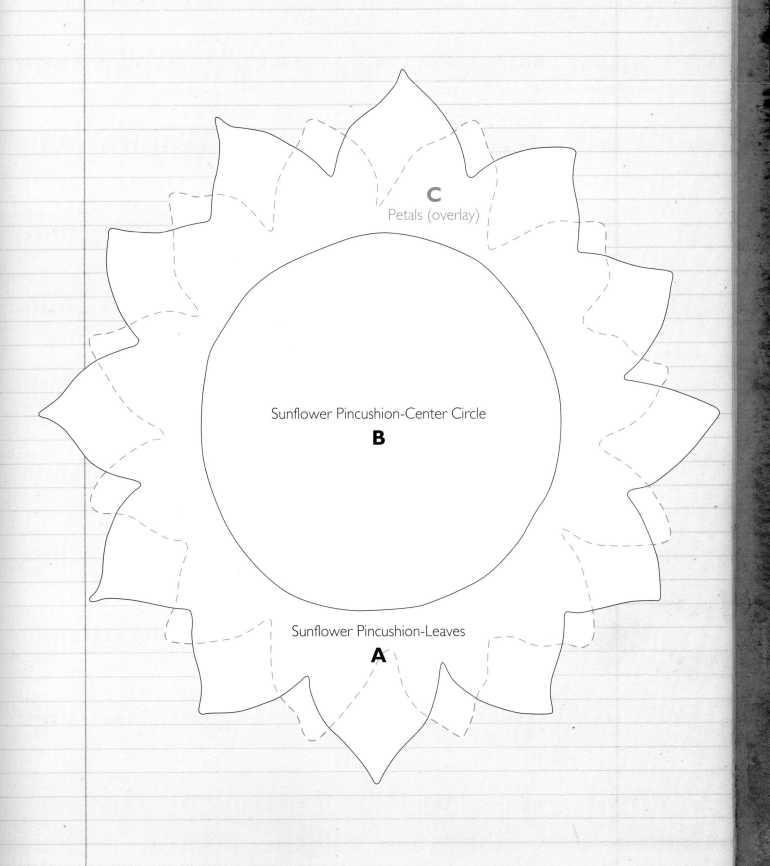

Petals (overlay)

C

Sunflower Pincushion-Center Circle

B

Sunflower Pincushion-Leaves

A

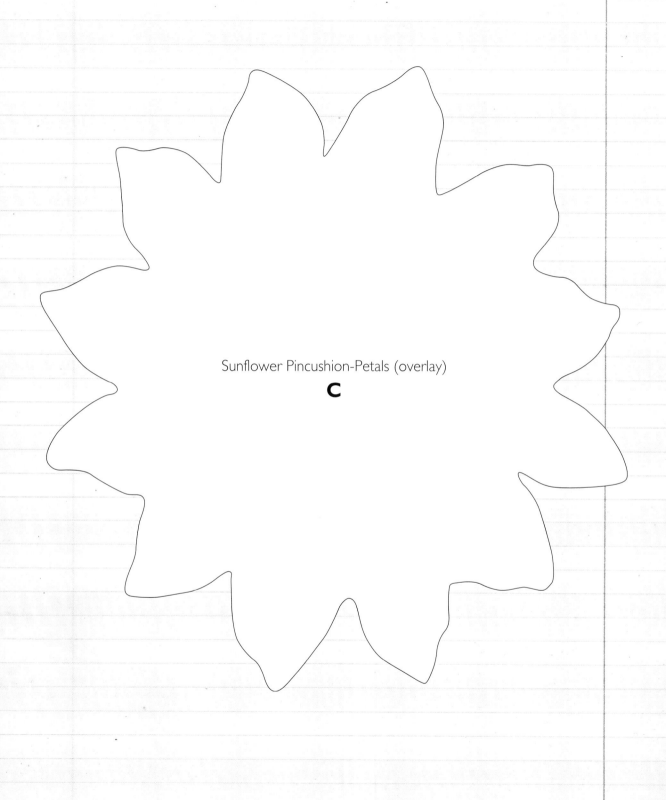

Sunflower Pincushion-Petals (overlay)

C

32

Anna Elizabeth Marshall

Elderly Anna. Photo courtesy of Grant Clothier

No 38.

A Dixie Rose Blooms

Anna Elizabeth Marshall, Civil War Bride

Born in 1851, Anna Elizabeth Marshall came to the prairie as a child in 1856. Fearing Civil War, her family — including six children — moved by covered wagon from Kentucky to Bates County, Missouri — five miles from the Kansas-Missouri state line. The turmoil of "Union or Sucesh?" (determining whether a person was a Union or Confederate sympathizer) was a way of life. Anna's father, Jonathan, was once kidnapped by Bushwackers, who stole his horses, but later freed him. Family members said he never talked about the incident. Further upheaval came in the wake of the 1863 raid of Lawrence by William Quantrill, which resulted in Order #11, forcing the relocation of all citizens living within 15 miles of the Kansas/Missouri state line. Many farms were looted and burned after the families left.

When the war ended in April 1865, the Marshall family moved back to Bates County and began rebuilding what was left of their farm. One year later, at the age of 15, Anna Marshall met James Byron Clothier, her future husband and father of her 17 children.

J. B. Clothier had enlisted in the Army in 1864, weeks shy of his 16th birthday. In 1866, his family relocated from Iowa and bought land adjoining the Marshall's in Bates County. J.B. and Anna courted for two years at neighborhood frolics, corn shuckings, and barn raisings. They married on Dec. 24, 1868, ages 20 and 17 respectively. Their young age was not unusual — in fact, many brides even married at age fourteen.

In 1874, with three children and expecting a fourth, the young Clothiers headed west to Kansas to claim 160 acres of land, which was allowed by the Homestead Act of 1862. The trip took three weeks, and almost everyone walked beside their wagons or rode horses to avoid the rough ride over poor roads.

Anna gave birth to her fourth child one week after the family arrived at their new home, Peace Creek. They prospered there, acquiring over 800 acres of land. Anna had 17 children in all, but only 15 survived to adulthood. Their marriage lasted 65 years. J.B. died in 1933 and Anna at age 97 in December of 1948.

Family letters and stories

While Anna's father, Jonathan Marshall, traveled down a Missouri road, moving a herd of his horses, bushwhackers rode up on him and demanded an answer to their question, "Union or Sucesh?" The meaning of this question is "Are you a Union loyalist or a Southern secessionist?"

Depending on who is asking the question or how one answered made the difference of losing your life or saving it. The gang of rebel bushwhackers kidnapped him and stole his horses. No one knows how Jonathan answered, but he lived and returned to his family unharmed.

Filmore, April 1st 1866

Dear Son,

I seat my self to write you a few lines. We are all well except bad colds. Father's health is not very good. Hard work has broke him down. I hope when this reaches you, you may be enjoying good health. I am afraid Bitey that you drink and gamble. You did not tell me for I have had a great deal of trouble about it. If you do, say you

36

Unknown woman wearing a bonnet over her parted hair, Civil War era. She wraps herself with a lovely Paisley shawl. Photo from the collection of Terry Thompson.

will never do so anymore and then stick to it.
Byron if you was here and see how some of the
boys act I think you would be ashamed.
Don't do it for my sake hear me once more if
you have any respect or love for me. We
will leave here in about 3 weeks. I don't
expect you can answer till we move to
our new home. We have had a
backward spring it is very muddy.
Byron I forgot to tell you that you have
a little brother six months old. It is getting dark
and my eyes are poor and I will quit by asking you to be a good boy and
remember what I have told you. I will write again before we leave here. I
want you to write to Uncle Matthew just as quick as you get this and maybe he
will get it before we pass there and then we can hear from you. We will go right
by there direct to Sullivan Co., Pennville, Mo. Do that as soon as you get this it is
so dark I cant see.

    Goodnight

    M.J. Clothier and J.B. Clothier

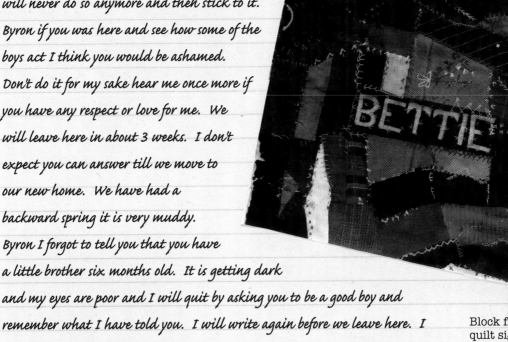

Block from friendship quilt signed by Anna with her nickname Bettie. Quilt block and photo courtesy of Betty Kinnamon.

    Byron your mother has been writing and has room for more to be written and I improve
the opportunity now presented. Providence we shall leave here in 20 days. We shall start
south into the state of Missouri and shall with little doubt cross the Missouri River before
stopping. I desire to go to a warmer climate. I shall leave this place worth about Six
Thousand Dollars. I have 2 teams of good horses and expect to get another. I had hoped you
could come home before we left. Time enough to of done some visiting and go with us but as
time approaches I have given it up. Should you not get home before we go and not before we
stop, I will write immediately where I am. I shall return here in the winter and you can
come out with me and make a visit and see your old playmates. I do this for the express
purpus of trying to keep you out of temptation to spend your time and money foolishly as many
of the boys have done since they come home, Byron. I have had a great deal of anxiety about
you on account of the many temptations (that) surround you. You may have been tempted to
gamble and lose your money and poison your mind. You may have been tempted to drink

intoxicating drinks and poison your mind and body both but if you have let me exhort you to stop and if you have acquired any other of all the vices that are around you stop them and be a man among men act a manly and an honorable part and improve your time in informing yourself. Do your duty be courteous to all and all will be courteous to you with very few exceptions. And now, my son be sober be watchful be diligent be courteous be faithful be patient be cheerful keep your body clean and you mind untainted with vice and your life will be pleasant and God will bless you and keep you from evil this is my earnest prayer.

Your father, C. Clothier

To my beloved son J.B. Clothier

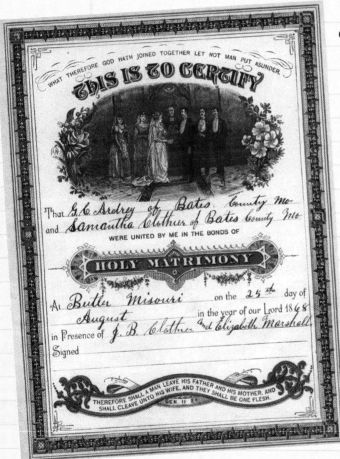

Most likely Anna wore her best cotton dress for the wedding ceremony, which was common for young women in a war economy. Fashion allowed a white silk bonnet, gloves and leather shoes if the family could afford it. Most frontier women chose practicality over high fashion, as the darker colors allowed the bride to wear the wedding dress for many years to all occasions. Women wore dresses made from a lightweight wool and cotton fabric, known as "delaine." The wool absorbed dyes much better than cotton and the stable delaine fabric refused to fade, thus retaining the same brightness in color for many years.

If a bride and groom married farther west on the prairie of Kansas, the following account describes the wedding setting of newlyweds repeating their marriage vows in less than favorable conditions.

Jessie Hill Rowland described one circa 1870's home-style wedding at which her father, a local justice of the peace, officiated: *"On one of those* occasions my father was asked to preside at a wedding ten miles away from home and my mother received an invitation to accompany him. Upon arriving at their destination they were ushered down six steps into a dugout, where the mother of the bride was preparing a wedding feast. There was but one room

Pioneers gather at the doorway of their dugout. Photo courtesy of Riley County Historical Society.

and the furniture consisted of two chairs, one with only two rungs to the back and bottomless. A bed made of scantlings, a board table, a short bench, a stove and a motto hung over the door, "God Bless Our Home."

"There was no flooring, and a sheet had been stretched across one corner of the room. The bride and groom were stationed behind this, evidently under the impression it would not be proper to appear until time for the ceremony." Mrs. Brown, we will call her, was grinding something in a coffee mill but arose to receive her guests with all the dignity of the first lady of the land. She placed one chair for my mother and one for my father; seating herself upon the bench, she continued turning the coffee grinder. Soon after some of the neighbors came in and at the appointed time the bride and groom emerged arm in arm from behind the temporary curtain and stepping forward to where my father was sitting, all became quiet and he pronounced the words that made them one.

"Soon after all sat down to the wedding supper. The sheet that hung across the corner of room was taken down and spread over the table for a cloth. Mrs. Brown's efforts at the coffee mill had turned out some delicious coffee, made of dried carrots. There were seven different kinds of sauce; all made out of wild plums put up in seven different ways. The rest of the menu was quite simple and consisted of plain bread and butter, and fried pork. The table was shoved close to the bed and three sat on that side while three sat on the bench. The chairs were occupied and two or three kegs finished out the number of seats."

Dixie Rose Crib Quilt

A quilt to honor Bettie

56" x 56"

I chose the Dixie Rose pattern to represent my chapter on Anna, my great-grandmother. Born in Kentucky, she needed a southern pattern. Some research turned up two quilts with the Dixie Rose quilt design. I liked the asymmetry of the pattern and the use of the paisley shapes for leaves. The paisley design in cotton and wool fabric remained popular throughout the 19th century. During the Civil War years, woven paisley shawls served as a warm wrap when folded into a triangle, nicely fitting over the hooped skirts of the day.

In keeping with the historical nature of the patterns I made my quilt in turkey red, chrome yellow, gold, and Victorian green — the bright color palette of 1845-1865.

Turkey red printed cotton fabric enjoyed great popularity with American quiltmakers from about 1830 to 1860. An expensive product imported from France, piecers and appliquérs trusted the turkey red dye process not to bleed into the white background of their quilts. Nearly all appliquéd quilts depended on this rich color, ranging from tomato red to a deep blue red, to represent their lovely appliquéd roses, tulips, coxcombs and berries. In unused early appliquéd and pieced quilts, the deep red remains unfaded. However, if the quilt required multiple washings, the color gently faded to pink.

Read through all directions before beginning this quilt.

Yardage

- 2 ½ yards ecru for background block and borders
- 2 yards green for stems, leaves, large rosette, small rosette, and border vines.
- 1 yard gold for reverse appliqué and reels
- 2 yards red
- ½ inch bias maker

Cutting and sewing

- Cut 4 large red roses D
- Cut 4 red buds E with short straight stem for block and 12 red buds with curved stems for borders
- Cut 5 large crowns B for corners and center rosette
- Cut 1 large green rosette A
- Cut 4 green circles J for corner reels
- Cut 5 gold reels C

- Cut 4 large green stems H
- Cut 8 leaves I
- Cut 24 large paisley leaves F
- Cut 12 small paisley leaves G

This block is made differently than the others.

- Cut out the 36 ½" square block first. Fold and press guidelines.
- Cut and sew the top and bottom borders 10 ½" x 36 ½". Cut and sew the side borders 10 ½" x 56 ½".
- I added the borders to the block first before I appliquéd the roses and vines so the border line could have a deeper dip into the border and spill over into the block.

Rosette assembly

All reels and buds are assembled and appliquéd as units before placing on quilt block. Begin with large 10" center rosette A. Pin the crown B to rosette A. Place crown points as shown in pattern. Next pin reel C to the middle of rosette A, centering and tucking the four ends under the crown B shown. Baste the three units, then appliqué by hand or machine.

Rosette A is not used for corner reels. Make a template of the circle J, add seam allowance. Place reel C on circle J, then place crown B over J and C. Baste and appliqué all four corner reels as units.

Roses and buds:

The sewing technique featured in this quilt is reverse appliqué. Don't be intimidated. Reverse appliqué simply means cutting a straight line in the top appliqué, revealing another fabric underneath, and appliquéing the raw edges of the cut line under ¼". This adds depth and interest to flowers and was utilized in many appliquéd quilts of the 19th century. To read more about how to reverse appliqué, see the Good Advice section at the back of the book.

- Prepare all roses and buds with the reverse appliqué method.
- Now that the rosettes, roses and buds are sewn, lay out the background block on a design wall and begin placing the large center rosette in the center of the block where all fold lines intersect. Pin in place.

- Next, lay out large stems H in a swirling direction as seen in the quilt picture. Pin in place.
- Place prepared units of roses, buds and leaves. Pin in place.
- When all appliqué pieces are placed correctly, baste in place, removing pins as you go.

Borders

- For the vine, cut four long one-inch bias strips of green.
- Pull strips through bias maker which automatically folds under the ¼" seam allowance to the center of the strip. See instructions on making a bias strip in the Good Advice section.
- Place and pin appliquéd corner reels in each corner.
- Referring to the quilt, gently curve the vine from the reel, down into the border then up again into the opposite reel. You can do this by eye. When vine looks right, pin in place.
- Place and pin the buds and leaves along vine, again referring to the quilt for placement.
- Place pinned quilt on design wall. Make any adjustments needed, then baste, removing pins as you go.
- Appliqué in place by hand or machine. Remove all basting threads when appliqué is finished.
- Quilting: Lori Kukuk echo-quilted around each appliqué, creating beautiful shadows in the background. She machine quilted Dixie Rose. Echo quilting looks great by hand or machine and does not require any marking. Just judge ¼" or more with your eye and follow the curves and shapes of the appliqué. Enjoy the process.
- Bind around edges.

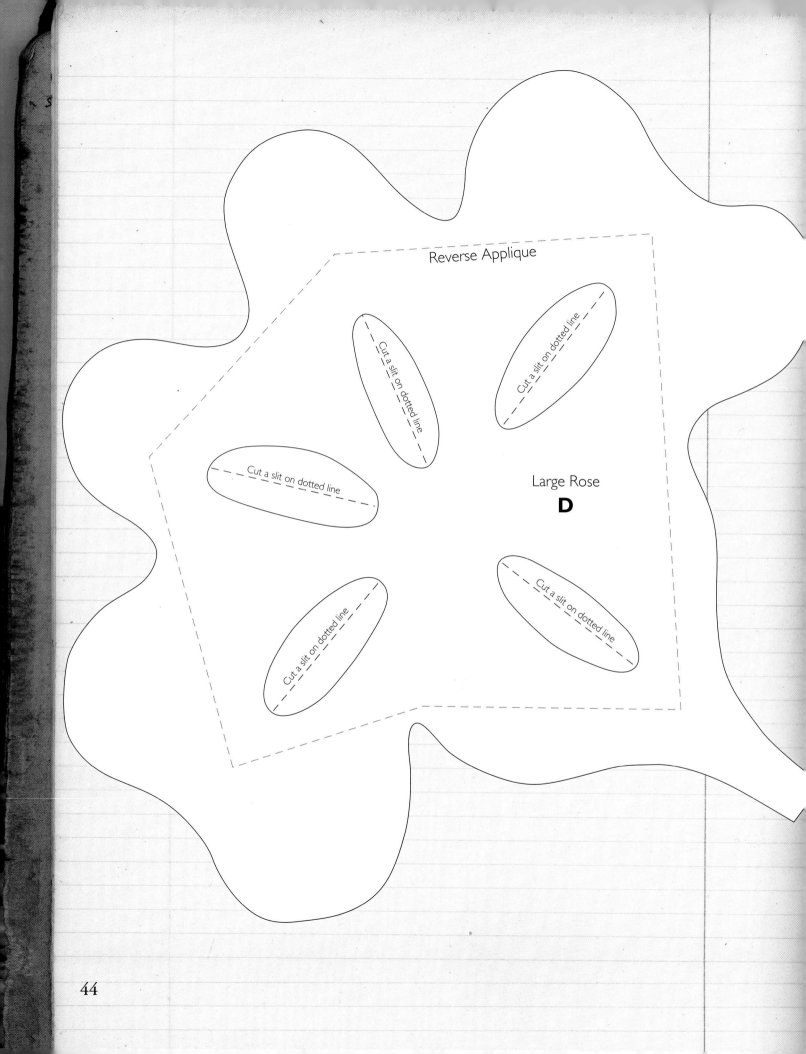

Reverse Applique

Cut a slit on dotted line

Cut a slit on dotted line

Cut a slit on dotted line

Large Rose
D

Cut a slit on dotted line

Cut a slit on dotted line

44

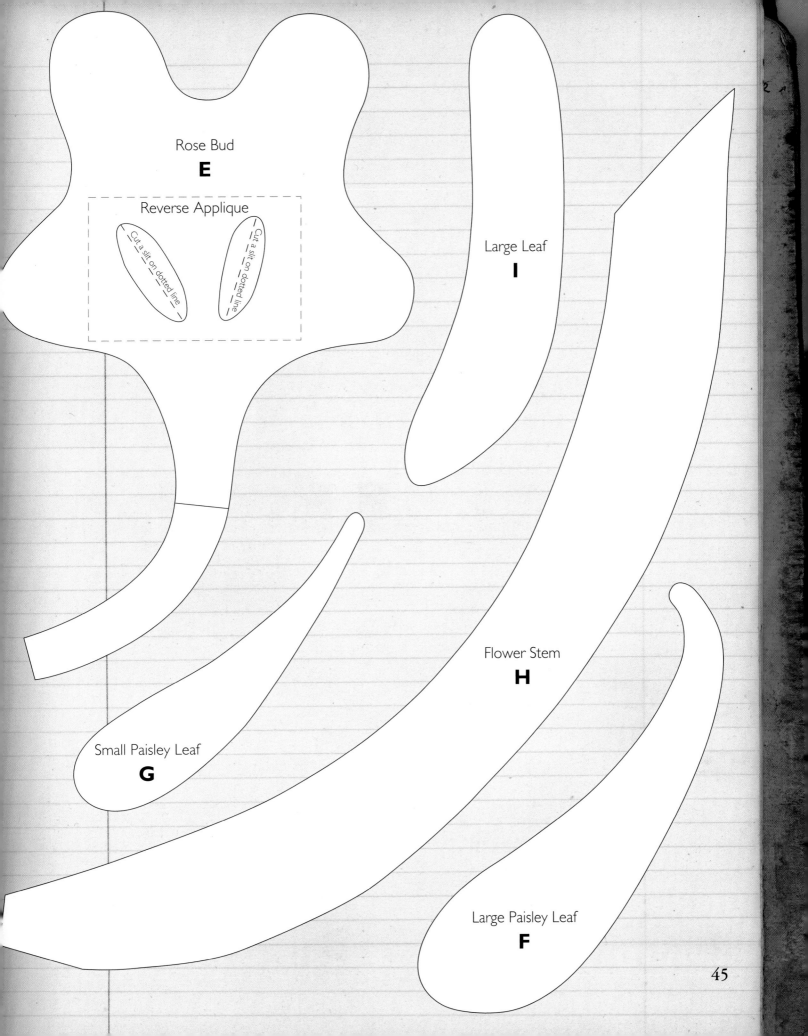

Rose Bud

E

Reverse Applique

Cut a slit on dotted line

Cut a slit on dotted line

Large Leaf

I

Flower Stem

H

Small Paisley Leaf

G

Large Paisley Leaf

F

45

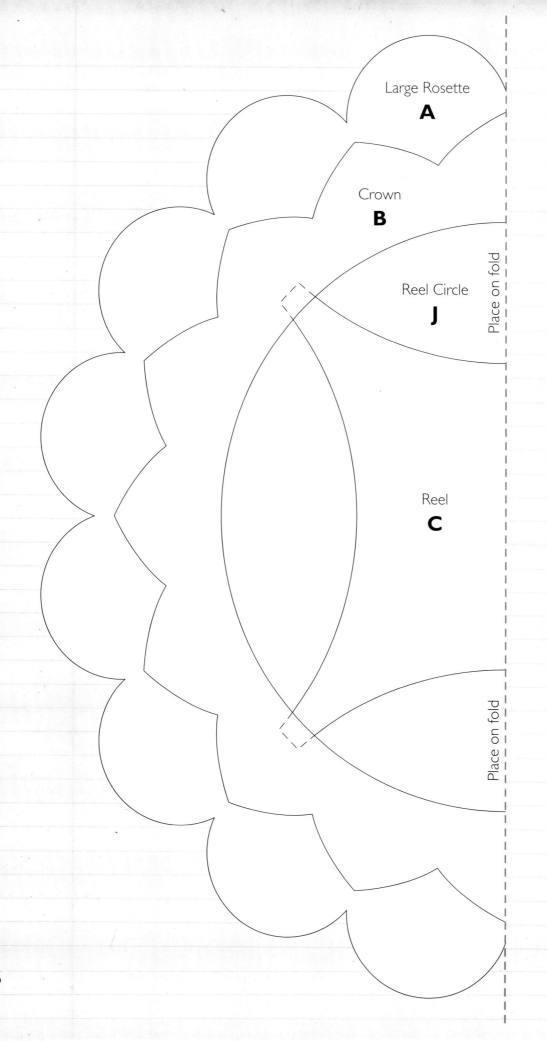

Large Rosette

A

Crown

B

Reel Circle

J

Reel

C

Place on fold

Place on fold

Anna's Apron

Women wore aprons to protect dresses from spills and splatters as they attended their household chores. This vintage apron sewn by machine was probably made c.1875-1890. It's simple and easy to make. Made of rectangles, one does not need a full size pattern to make the apron. The square bib and collar are one piece with a hole cut for placing over the head. The bottom of the bib is tightly gathered at the waist. You may adjust the gathering to fit.

Bib

- Cut bib rectangle 17" x 23".
- Turn ¼" seam allowance under twice to finish the edges.
- Lengthen or shorten bib to adjust to your neckline and waistline.
- Cut a 9 ½" circle for head, 4 ½" from top of rectangle.

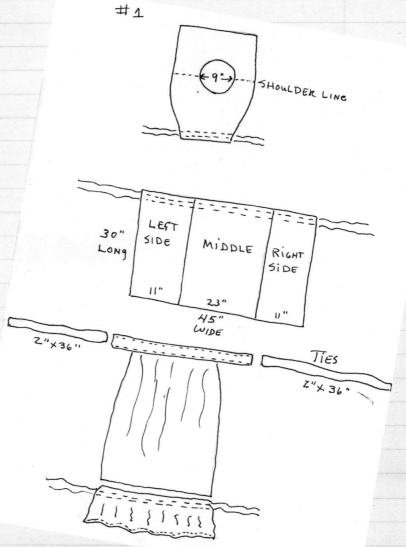

Skirt

- The gathered skirt measures 45" wide and 30" long.
- The skirt is made in three sections.
- Add ½" seam allowance to each side section and turn ¼" seam allowance under twice to finish edges.
- Sew skirt sections together.
- Stitch two gathering lines ¼" apart on top of apron, ¼" from raw edge of top skirt of apron.

Waistband

- Cut a 2" strip 30"* long. (*Note: The band on the vintage apron was pinned to clothing in the back. To make ties, add 1 yard to each end of tie before you sew band to skirt.) Sew strip onto gathered skirt marking the centers of waistband and skirt.
- Sew band right sides together, then turn band right sides out. Press, topstitch all edges.
- Make bottom ruffle with two strips each 40" x 5". Gather to fit bottom of apron skirt. Finish edges.

Bess Corey

A Single Woman Goes West

Bess Corey

"I tell you pioneer life didn't end in the long ago — it's a fright the way some poor wretches have to live. I am very fortionate and can live up to my motto "Do all the good you can to all the folks you can in all the ways you can and smile, darn you, smile." And the worse my luck the more fun I make of it and folks who come with long faces to sympathize go home laughing and saying "What fer a schoolma'am we got this year anyway[?]"

Iowa-born Bess Corey stood 5'7" and weighed 180 pounds — considered a large woman in the early 1900s. Her personality and pluck proved even larger as Bess began to make her way alone in the world. The death of her father at age 17 pushed her out of the overcrowded family farmhouse and into the world. She finished ninth grade and became certified to teach school in Iowa.

Bess followed the dream of many settlers: the Homestead Act that offered free land to anyone who staked a claim and lived on the land for five years. With a little money saved from teaching, 21-year-old Bess took a train and set out for Midland, South Dakota, in 1909. She passed the South Dakota teaching exams and immediately staked her own 160 acres of land in Stanley

County, with the dream of building a stock farm of horses and cattle, and a little grain farming.

These were remarkable achievements for a single woman in those days. In addition to that, Bess was a writer. Her outlet for that was hundreds of letters she wrote to her family in Iowa in her first decade out west. She wrote in great detail about her adventures as a "schoolma'am" and homesteader. She described the land, her claim shack, her homesickness, her school, and students, her friends — both men and women — and their social gatherings. Her letters reflected her great sense of humor, the ironies of her situation, her courage, and her positive attitude for living and maintaining her humor in difficult times.

Bess researched the available land before she chose the spot to stake her claim, then she traded it for better land. With no available cash, she negotiated with the local lumberman for materials for her new house—a 12' x 16' structure — and a neighbor to build it.

Her schoolma'am duties called for her to rise at 5:30 a.m. every morning, and walk two miles to her schoolhouse, build a fire in the stove, and wait for her students to arrive. Their numbers varied from 12 to 20 children and young adults.

"My school will begin Sept. 6th and close Dec. 26th for eight weeks of vacation during the bad part of the winter. It begins again Feb. 21st and closes June 10th. I will have fifteen or twenty pupils, several of whom are young men of Fuller's age (Bess's younger brother, by two years) or nearly that — hence the ninth grade."

Bess's letters mention sewing for herself and for neighbors and friends. She made aprons, embroidered a coat, sewed waists (blouses), and made comforters out of feed sacks. She loved her little home and spent evenings cleaning and sewing.

"Yesterday afternoon I made three pillow slips and today I made another pair of bloomers — have one of the mittens knit for Ruthie's doll," she wrote.

Even with all her work and effort to survive on her own, Bess found time to socialize and be with men and women she liked. They went to dances, where she wore out her shoes and danced until dawn. Taffy pulls and picnics kept her social life full of fun, and her popularity brought her many marriage proposals. She never fell in love or met a mate who suited her. She wrote home about the cowboys and the women of South Dakota:

Dist 19

Bethlehem School Fulton Children

Students in District 19, Bethlehem School. Photo courtesy of Belleville Kansas Historical Society

"Gee I wish you were out here to drive away the men — darn 'em. The wemon say 'You'll have to let 'em love you up a little or you'll never get along in Dakota' but I can't bring myself to it. There is one old fool here who is gone on me and was telling Mrs. Reese about it. She told me and I don't know how I'll ever shake him off… The wemon all swear here till it makes the chills run down my back, must close soon[,] your sister Bess.

P.S. I notice that my spelling is fierce but if you can make it out [, then it's] alright."

At the age of 38, the South Dakota Board of Education required Bess to earn a high school degree so she could continue teaching. She left her ranch and enrolled in the Fort Pierre High School where her classmates were the age of her own students. She continued to teach in South Dakota until shortly before her death in 1954.

— To read more of Bess Corey's letters from South Dakota, look for the book "Bachelor Bess: The Homesteading Letters of Elizabeth Corey 1909-1919", edited by Phillip L. Gerber. It's available from the University of Iowa Press, http://www.uiowa.edu/uiowapress/gerbacbes.htm. Our quotes are taken from this book.

"I was sick most all day yesterday and last night and didn't get up till most ten o'clock today. Then I got something to eat and finished off that comforter around the edge. Gee! it's a "whopster"—so big and soft and warm—has about eight pounds of cotton in it."

"You folks think you know something about cold weather but you don't. I had got used to having my hair, eyebrows and eyewinkers covered with frost and ice till I looked like Santa Clause when I got to school but Sun. night beat that all hollow. I went to bed with the covers over my head and just a little air hole over my right eye and when I woke up in the night I found when I put up my hand to turn down the covers that my hair and the blanket were covered with hoar frost."

This is a deluxe claim shack. Bess' was the size of the right portion only. Photo from the collection of Terry Thompson.

"Since I came home I've melted snow, done a big washing, finished my comfort around the edge and covered the partition between the sittingroom and kitchen with heavey building paper. Was to have gone back to Speers tonight for the rest of the week but there's so much to do here. I want to iron and scrub, sew my carpet and put it down, take a bath, scrub my hair, make out my reports and do some mending. Would like to go to town one day this week if possible."

"I sewed my carpet and put it down Saturday — am working on a rug now between times. It is getting so cozy and homelike here I cant stand it, hardly[,] to be away long. This last time I was so homesick at times that I hardly knew whether I was a foot or a horseback."

54

"You must not worry about any thing I write — the cowboys are mostly a pretty good sort — all except a few like Sunshine — the way they propose to a girl — they ride up to her door — draw a six shooter and say "Wilt thou[?]" and she wilts. One girl was engaged to a man back east so she didn't wilt and he shot her — her folks were rich and went after him and he got to be a manager in the shirt factory for two years — he won't get out for a year yet and Sunshine has eloped with another man's wife so guess I'll get along alright.

Much obliged for the box, hope I get it soon — Please write Your Little Girl Bess"

"When folks here get land broke and raise their living they live fat but poor people who haven't much breaking done have to scratch. I'm a lucky dog though — I have an eight months school instead of six and may get $45 instead of $40 so you don't need to bother about me at all. I'll not have to suffer as lots of people do in this new country."

"The other day I cleaned the school house — swept down the walls and ceiling, washed the windows, black-boards, desks, seats, wash stand, scrubbed the floor and porch. The floor I scrubbed first with a broom then got down on my knees and went over it — quite a job but I felt hardly tired when I got through and my shoulder hardly ached a bit."

"I worked like a slave till nine o'clock then after a supper of sardines and crackers I went to roost. Seldom has a meal tasted better to me than that first one in the new house. I worked as hard as I could all day last Sunday and didn't have things half straight then. The next five mornings I was up at half past five or before and it keeps me bussy then to wash, dress, comb my hair, get my breakfast and be ready for school at seven. I like to have my school fire built by eight. When it is stormy I have to start for school in the dark. I faced the storm Monday morning and went in knee deep a good bit of the way then the wind shifted and I had to face it going home that night. Speers thought sure I would come home with the children and when they got home without me they sent one of the boys after me...."

She signed most of her letters Yours, Bachelor Bess.

"At last [my brother Fuller] told someone that he thought it a wonder that I, a girl along among strangers, had done so well — better than most of the men had done."
— Elizabeth Corey, 1911

55

Bess's Schoolma'am quilt

"I'm a lucky dog"

46" x 61 1/2"

Fabric for Bess' Quilt

I used a black and red ticking for the background blocks. In 1900, ticking was used extensively for mattresses and pillows. Since Bess was so colorful, I chose bright, clear colors against a black and red-striped background.

Yardage

- 1 ½ yard black/red ticking (cut into (4) 18" x 26" rectangles). Finished blocks are 17 ½" x 25 ½".
- 2 yds for borders, sashing
- ⅛ yd. scraps of light blue/green, yellow, pink, brown plaid for flowers, birds, dragonfly, horse, etc.
- ¼ yd. each of 3 greens for leaves
- ¼ yd. each of 6 reds for flowers, hearts
- ⅛ yd. each of yellow, gold, ticking, checks and stripes for pots.
- Cotton thread to match appliquéd shapes.

Appliqué Blocks

- Follow directions for hand or machine appliqué preparation.
- Cut (4) background blocks 18" x 26".
- Arrange pots, flowers, hearts and all designs in a free, random way around the rectangle block.
- Follow the picture as a guide.
- I think the top running stitch would look great on this primitive quilt.
- Baste in place. Appliqué by hand or machine.

Setting blocks

- Cut (2) 3" x 18" sashing strips to set blocks 1 and 3, and blocks 2 and 4.
- Cut (1) long strip 3" x 54"
- Sew the middle 3" x 54" strip between the two halves of the quilt.

Setting borders

- For top and bottom border, cut (2) strips 4 ½" x 38".
- Sew to top and bottom of quilt.
- For side borders, cut 4 ½" x 62".
- Sew to sides of quilt. Quilt should measure 46" x 61 ½".

- Outline and echo quilt around each appliqué, as shown. You might also want to draw around each appliqué template in the empty spaces and quilt the birds, flowers, dragonfly or heart shapes to fill the space. The top running stitch by hand or machine is a fitting way to appliqué these folk designs. Use black or red thread so the stitches show.

The folk appliqué designs came from an old turn-of-the-century red and green pieced quilt. The quilt was quilted by treadle machine in these delightful designs of flowers, hearts, insects and pots. The quiltmaker quilted each block separately, then sewed the quilted blocks together. The back of the quilt is a separate calico backing. The "quilt as you go" method is not so new after all.

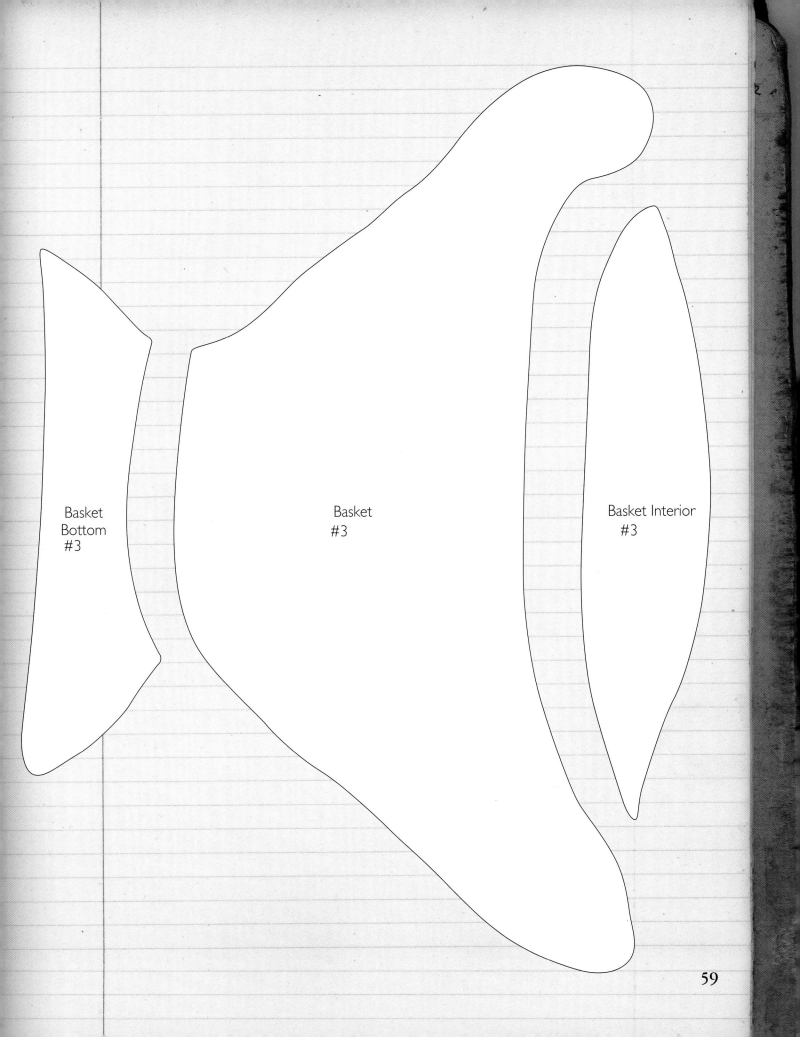

Basket
Bottom
#3

Basket
#3

Basket Interior
#3

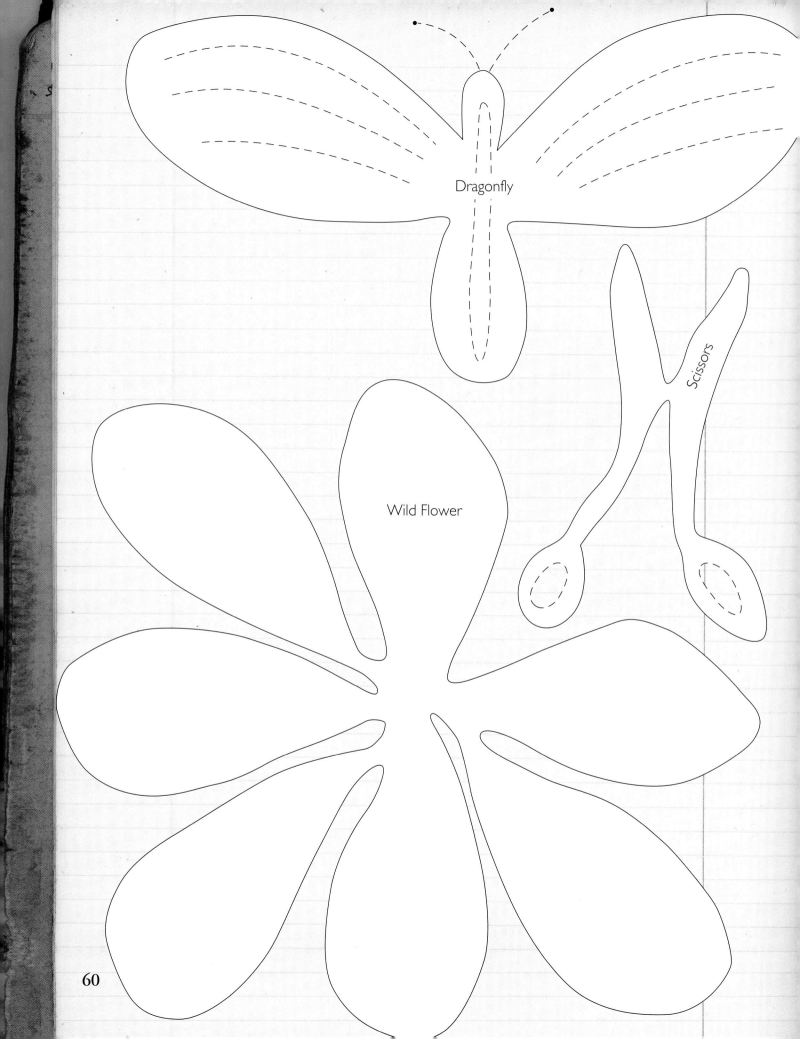

Dragonfly

Scissors

Wild Flower

60

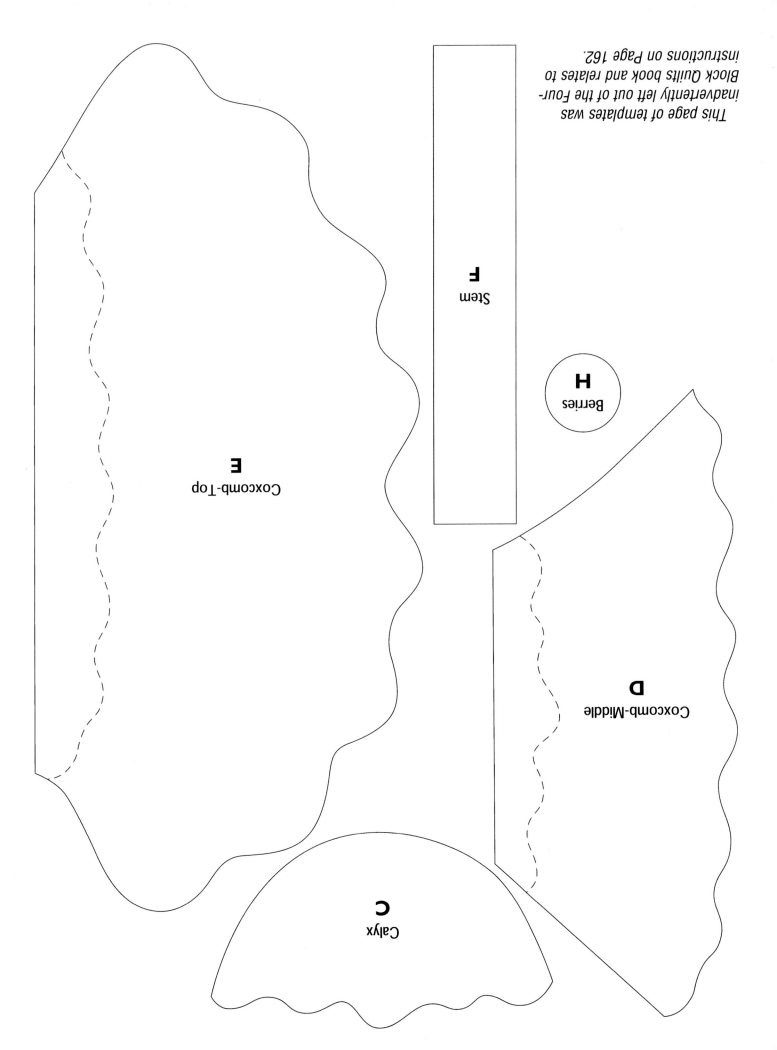

This page of templates was inadvertently left out of the Four-Block Quilts book and relates to instructions on Page 162.

F
Stem

H
Berries

E
Coxcomb-Top

D
Coxcomb-Middle

C
Calyx

Stems & Leaves
#2

Stems & Leaves
#1

61

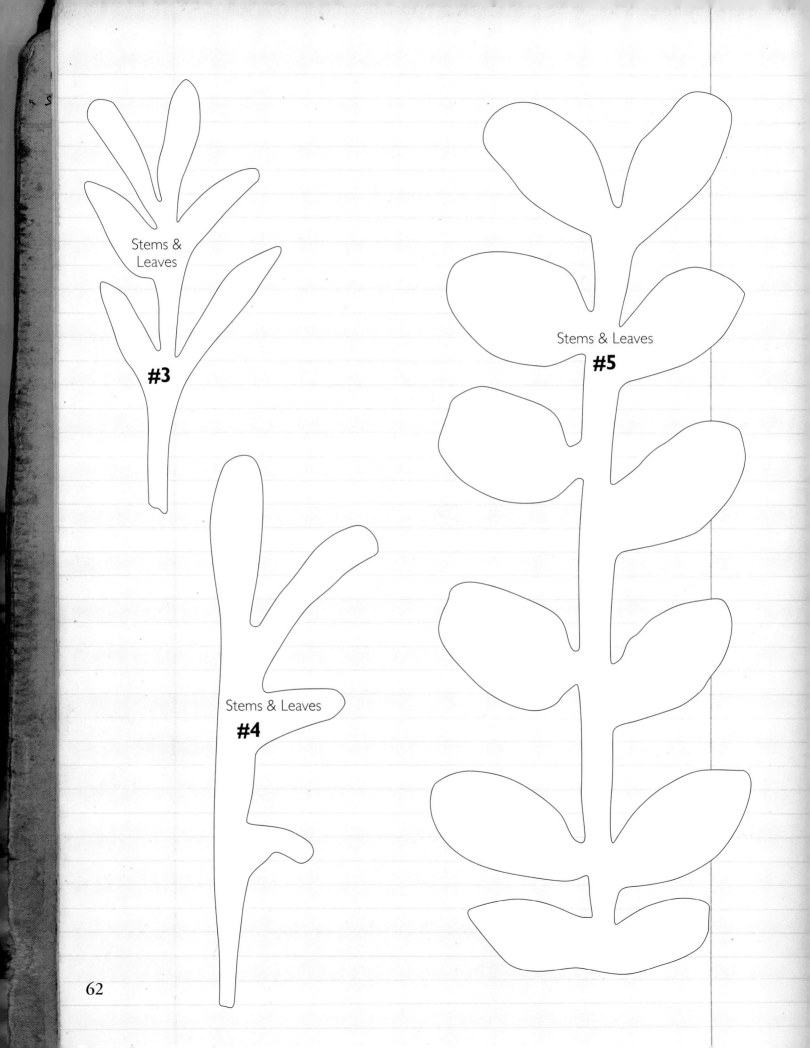

Stems &
Leaves

#3

Stems & Leaves
#4

Stems & Leaves
#5

Bird on a Branch
#1

Flower Center

Flower

Bird
#2

Kites

Bird
#3

63

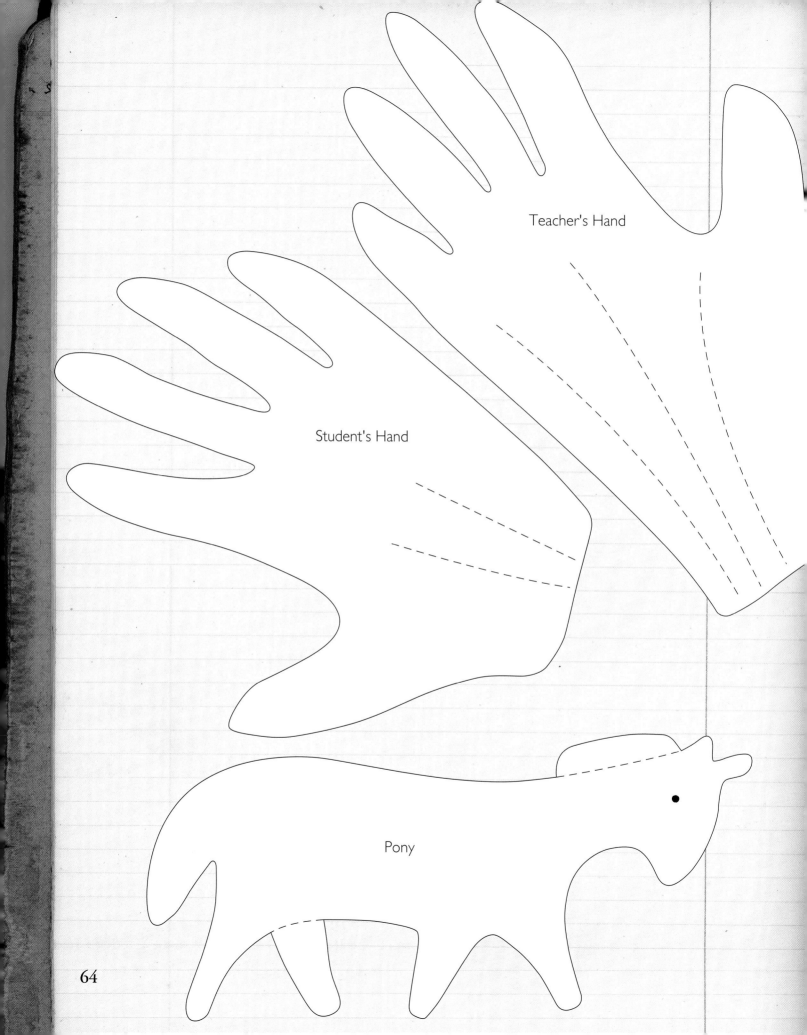

Teacher's Hand

Student's Hand

Pony

64

Flower

School Bell

Star

Moon

School Book

65

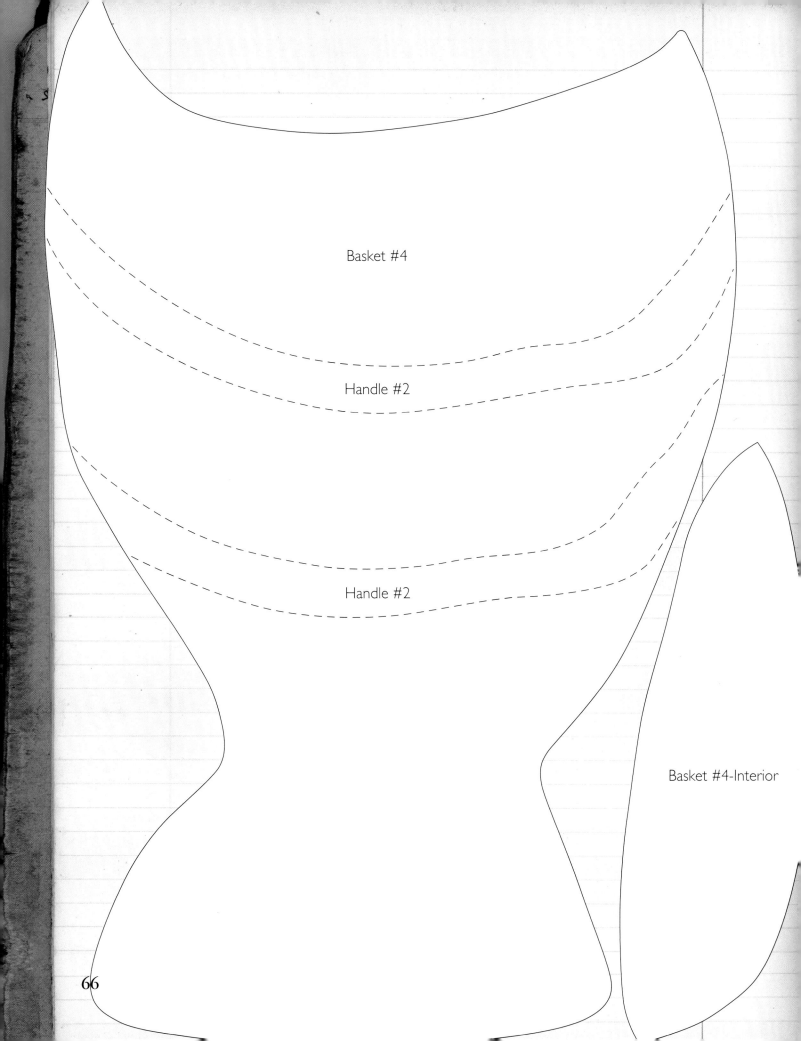

Basket #4

Handle #2

Handle #2

Basket #4-Interior

66

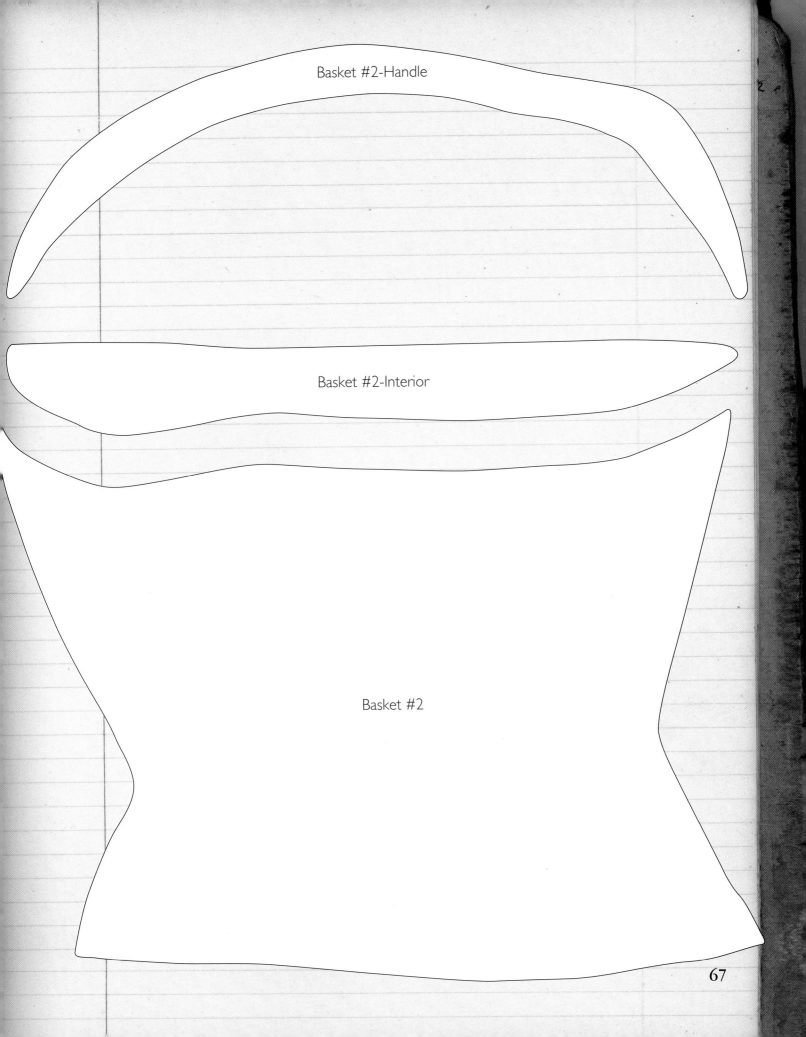

Basket #2-Handle

Basket #2-Interior

Basket #2

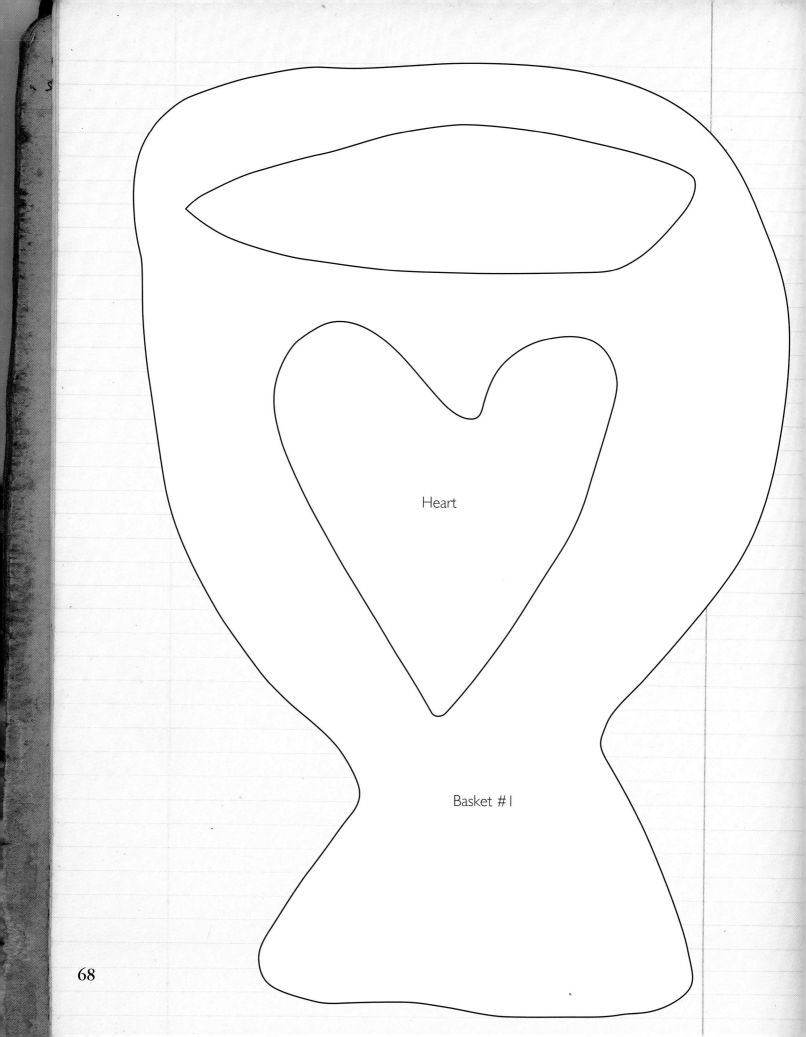

Heart

Basket #1

A Child's Redwork Sampler

Circa 1900

14" x 14"

Yardage/materials

- ½ yd. white or ecru good quality, permanent pressed muslin.

  Cut (16) 4" squares.
- 1-2 skeins of DMC red embroidery floss
- Small embroidery hoop

This small 16-block sampler was probably stitched by a child, as a "learn to embroider" project. Redwork or bluework embroidered table runners, quilts, baby bibs, pillow shams, and samplers occupied the hands of children and adults from 1890-1920.

The motifs of children at play, animals, birds and everyday objects were traced onto plain white 4" squares, then embroidered with an outline stitch with two strands of embroidery floss. Sometimes the maker signed her name—this sampler is signed by May. We also find Grandma's name on the flower block and the dog block. The work on the flower looks more experienced than the other pictures so perhaps "May" signed "Grandma" to practice making letters, or to distinguish her grandma's work.

After you have embroidered and signed and dated your 16-block sampler, sew the little blocks into four rows of four blocks. Quilt around the shapes or leave them unquilted as our little friend May chose to do. Sew a backing and present it to a new baby.

Grandma

May

Grandma

72

Children
of the Prairie

Two children pose with a Rocky Road quilt.
Courtesy, Shiloh Museum of Ozark History.

Children of the Prairie

This chapter celebrates two children who recorded their childhood pioneer adventures.

Arthur Cline Thompson wrote in his daily journal about his family's journey to Canada in a covered wagon. His short entries note his mother's grief. He hunts, fishes, and cooks meals for the family on the road to a new life.

Grace McCance Snyder had three dreams as she grew up in Nebraska. "I wished that I might grow up to make the most beautiful quilts, marry a cowboy and look down on the top of a cloud." All three came true. She made award-winning quilts, married cowboy Bert Snyder and flew in a plane to New York when her quilts were featured at the International Exposition in 1950.

Arthur's journal

Journal entries were made as Arthur's family traveled from Nebraska to Canada May 24 -August 21, 1897. Arthur (born in 1885) was 12.

In Wyoming, June 24 — A man with a horse and cart stopped here. He is on his way to Oregon. He will stay over and travel with us for a ways. He stopped, he said, because he heard Ma's canary's singing. And it has been a long time since he had heard such pretty sounds.

June 25 — It has rained and misted nearly all day. This afternoon travelers came by. They have three wagons. Asked about the road ahead, had some coffee, then went on. They too admired Ma's canary birds and tried to buy one but Ma, she wouldn't see.

July 2 — We broke camp about noon and drove 15 miles, camped on Wolf Creek. The grass is very poor but there is plenty of fire wood. I caught some nice trout for supper. Ma is not feeling well so I will fix it.

August — Traveled about 29 miles. Camped close to a store and post office, with the name of Crossfield. Ma sure is unhappy. This morning for the first time we didn't hear the canary birds singing. Looked in the cages and all three birds were dead. Killed by a mouse. She has cried all day. Poor Ma, and we were so close to the end of our trip. Pa said as soon as we get to Ida's he will get her some more birds.

Afterward — The canary bird cages rode in the wagon during the day, out of the sun. At night, they were covered and set on the wagon seat. The mouse that killed them was found in the horse feed bin at the back of the wagon. Needless to say the mouse didn't finish the trip either

Grace's story

Grace McCance Snyder grew up in a one-room sod house in the sandhills of western Nebraska. A tomboy, she preferred wearing demin pants to long calico dresses and also preferred working outdoors with her father, "Poppie." Nine-year-old Grace spent long days in the hills watching cattle, with only her dog as a companion. Her older sister Florry worked with their mother Margaret on the everyday tasks of cooking, washing clothes, cleaning, gardening, and preserving food.

"One evening, after the longest, lonesomest day yet, I watched Mama setting tiny,

quick stitches into the diamond-shaped calico scraps she was sewing into a Lone Star quilt top. And right then I knew what I wanted to do. I asked her for some pieces to sew while I sat in the strawstack all day, but she said I was too young to do a good job. I knew I wasn't, and I just had to have those pieces. I begged hard and promised to be ever so careful, and she finally said I could try a little Four Patch. "But you'll have to do neat work and fasten the ends of your thread good," she said, "for I can't afford to waste thread and pieces on you if you don't.

She cut the little squares and showed me how to put them together in the pattern. After that, when the sun had warmed the air enough that I could take my mittens off, I sat in my straw nests and sewed on the little quilt, making my stitches small and neat so Mama would let me have more pieces. Young as I was, I knew that Mama's needlework, even her patching, was extra fine, and that it wouldn't be easy to learn to sew as well as she did. But it was during those days in the big strawstack, when I worked so hard to keep my stitches even and the block corners matched, that I began to dream of the time when I could make quilts even finer than Mama's, finer than any others in the world."

Reading diaries and collecting pictures of women who made their homes as comfortable as possible, I notice that they often mention the threat and fear of rattlesnakes. Many young toddlers were confined to the house while the older children searched the yard for rattlers. Women record dramatic stories of pet dogs or chickens and sometimes a child being bitten and killed by these venomous snakes.

Another curious observation in early photographs of families posed in front of their sod houses is that one or two bird cages hung from the eaves near the door. Many women kept canaries for company during long lonely days of prairie living. Songbirds provided

A pretend quilting party. Photo from the collection of Terry Thompson.

another voice in song for women leading a harsh life. Their bright yellow feathers also gave a spot of color in the often drab surroundings of a dark home interior. Grace's daughter Billie, now 92, said the color of their feathers was as cheering as their singing.

Grace's mother Margaret owned a pair of yellow canaries, and she became quite attached to them. Perhaps they reminded her of her comfortable Missouri home where life was much easier and genteel. Margaret's mother, Grandma Blaine, faithfully sent three barrels of goods to her Nebraska pioneer family for Thanksgiving. One barrel held fresh apples from their Missouri orchard, another held molasses, and a third contained nuts, sweet potatoes, and special bundles for Margaret and her girls. Each girl received a dress length of calico.

Below, this china pattern, manufactured by the Salem China Company of Ohio, inspired Grace's mosaic-style quilt. Grace contacted the company for permission to use the design. In return, she received not only permission but also a complete set of the china.

"We would hang over Mama while she unwrapped Grandma's bundle, for out of it came a dress length of new calico for each of us. Every year Grandma cut each piece a little longer to accommodate our lengthening legs, and every second year she added a new piece for the baby girl who had learned to walk since she sent the last assortment. But better yet was Aunt Ollie's bundle of stylish hand-me-downs, her last year's jackets, dresses, and petticoats that Mama made over for us every winter. We always spread the lovely things out on the bed and made a big ceremony of looking at their rich colors, feeling their fine textures, and smelling their delicate perfumes. Then we divided them up. Florry had first pick the first year, I had it the second, and so on down the line.

Flower Basket Petit Point Quilt, 1942-43, pieced cotton, 92" x 94". By Grace McCance Snyder, Lincoln County, Nebraska This quilt, containing 85,789 pieces and 5,400 yards of thread, was made in 16 months. Photo courtesy of Nebraska Historical Society.

The soddy and the canaries too. The man and woman standing far right are Graces' parents. Grace is second from the left on the bench in the front row. Photo courtesy of Billie Lee Snyder Thornburg.

My new calico, that second year on the homestead was a lovely piece, black, sprigged all over with tiny green leaves and red dots, and I liked it better than any dress I ever had. We wore the new dresses Christmas Day, when Tottens and Yoders came to our house for dinner."

Grace faithfully pieced her quilts and on a trip to town with her mother, and she went to a new level of her quiltmaking career.

"I bought the things I needed. Then I used the last dollar of the money I had borrowed to go to school on to buy enough yard goods to piece a quilt top. I had been helping Mama piece quilts from scraps left over from our dressmaking, but this would be the first one I had ever made for myself, or from whole goods. I could hardly wait to get started on it — and I had no idea, that day, what a lifesaver it would be before the winter was over."

In her adult years, Grace accomplished her three wishes from childhood.

"I wished that I might grow up to make the most beautiful quilts in the world, to marry a cowboy, and to look down on the top of a cloud."

Grace Snyder lived to be 100 years old by 1982 and she is recognized as one of the most talented quiltmakers of the 20th century. To learn more about her life, told in her own words to her daughter, Nellie Snyder Yost, read "No Time on my Hands," published by the University of Nebraska Press. All quotations above are from their book.

Grace Snyder's Rose Wreath

"I Want to Marry a Cowboy"

58" x 58"

Yardage

- 5 yards neutral for blocks and borders
- 1¼ yd. red for small rose C and rose bud A
- ⅝ yd. pink for large rose G
- ⅛ yd. of (3) greens for leaves E, calyx B, and wreath F
- ½ yd. green bias for vine
- Scrap of yellow for rose centers
- ½ yd. blue for baskets
- ⅛ yd. red for baskets

Cutting Directions

- Cut 32 rose buds A
- Cut 32 calyx B
- Cut 20 small rose C
- Cut 20 rose center D
- Cut 64 leaves E
- Cut 16 wreath F
- Cut 20 pink large rose G

Basket Templates

- Cut 4 template A
- Cut 4 reverse, 4 template B
- Cut 32 blue C
- Cut 16 blue and 24 red D
- Cut 4 handle E

Center blocks

- Cut (4) 20½" x 20½" squares for background blocks.
- Follow the appliqué directions for hand or machine appliqué (see Good Advice).
- Arrange stems, roses calyx and buds. Follow the picture as a guide.
- Pin all in place. Baste and appliqué.
- Sew the four blocks together.

Borders

- Piece four basket blocks.
- The basket blocks measure 9" finished. Cut the 2 side borders 9½" x 16" and sew to each side of the basket block. Repeat for the second side border.
- Cut the top and bottom borders 9½" x 25" and sew to each side of 9½" basket block.
- Attach borders to your four block quilt.

- Follow the Vine Line directions (see Good Advice) for making the vines using a medium curve or use the curve pattern provided.
- Mark lines on both sides of the basket block beginning in the middle of the basket.
- Prepare bias vines by cutting (8) 1" x 29" strips of green bias. Refer to Good Advice for bias preparation.
- Begin each vine with the raw edge in the middle of the basket. The raw edges will be covered by two leaves.
- Place bias vines on pencil lines and pin vine in place out to the corner.

The ends of meeting vines are covered with (4) large rosettes.

- Place (4) bud/calyx units and (6) leaves per border. Pin and baste all appliqués.
- Appliqué by hand or machine.
- Appliqué large rosettes over ends of vines in each corner.
- Quilt a 7" Princess Feather Wreath in the center of each appliquéd wreath.
- Echo quilt around buds, leaves and stems on blocks and borders. Fill in empty spaces between blocks and borders with a feather vine.
- Bind quilt.

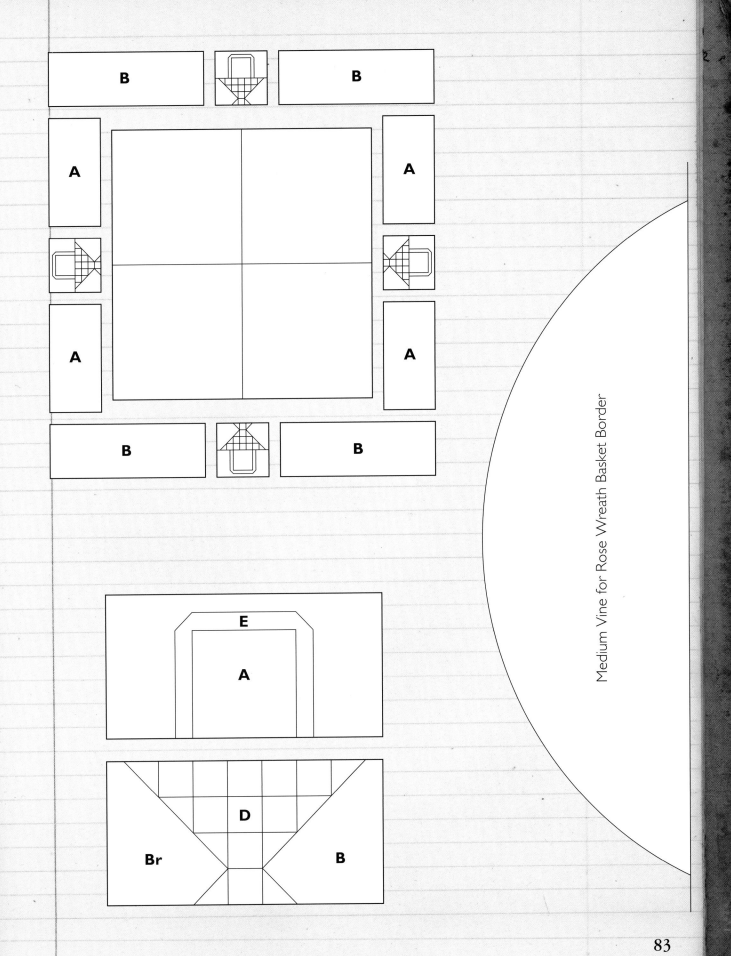

Medium Vine for Rose Wreath Basket Border

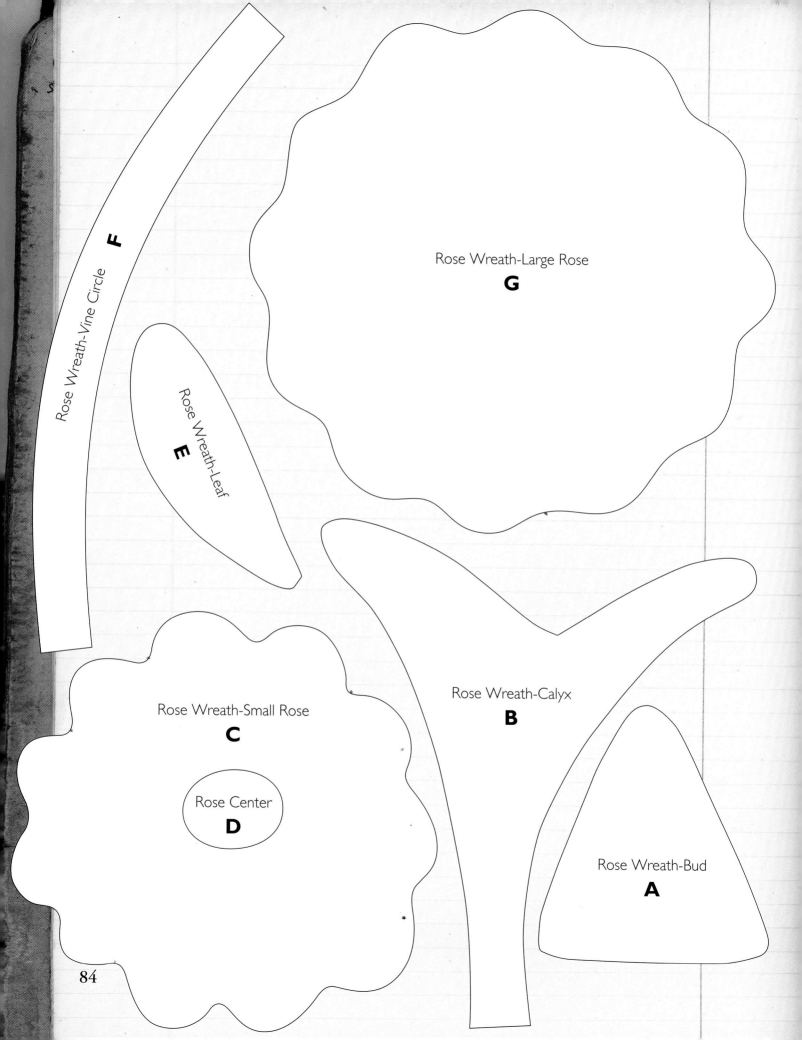

Rose Wreath-Vine Circle

F

Rose Wreath-Large Rose

G

Rose Wreath-Leaf

E

Rose Wreath-Calyx

B

Rose Wreath-Small Rose

C

Rose Center

D

Rose Wreath-Bud

A

84

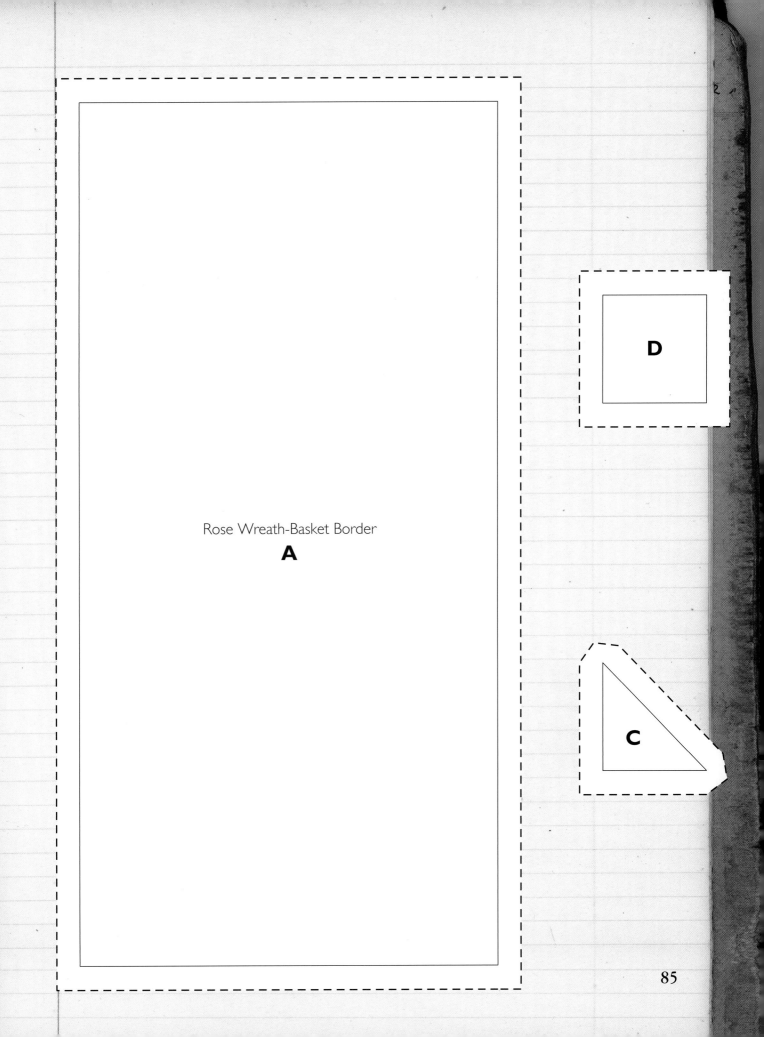

Rose Wreath-Basket Border
A

D

C

Rose Wreath-Basket Border
E

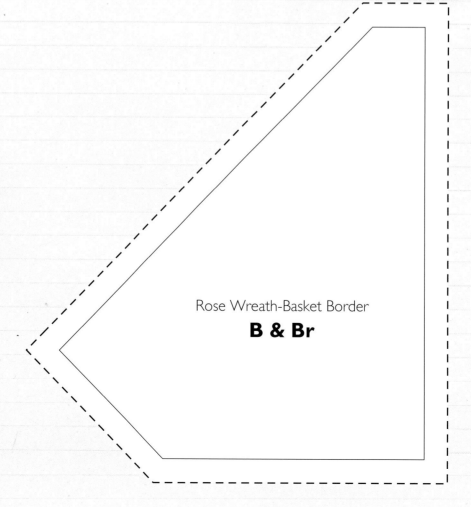

Rose Wreath-Basket Border
B & Br

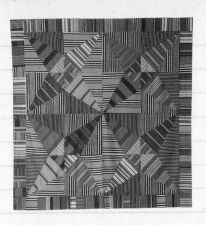

Rocky Road to Kansas

"We are so close to the end of our trip"

48" x 48"

What an appropriate name for a pioneer pattern. The road was rocky and dusty, full of holes--if there was a road at all. Wagons followed the paths and wheel-made ruts of previous travelers from 1840 to 1900. Finding it a rough ride in the wagon, most women and children walked the trail. Those who couldn't walk--the elderly and very young--endured the wagons.

The Rocky Road to Kansas pattern commemorates the journey west and is most often pieced with strips of calico or wool strips laid over the long triangle and stitched in a crazy quilt style. The unplanned pattern also represents the many crooked paths and obstacles that confronted travelers. Pioneers loaded their wagons with warm bedding in preparation for long and cold winters that lay ahead. I choose ticking for my Rocky Road quilt. It looks both traditional and yet contemporary. Enjoy the journey.

Read through all instructions before beginning.

Background yardage (background total: 2 yards)

- ½ yard each of two navy fabrics for background C
- 1 yard of royal blue for background C

Ticking yardage -

I chose blue, yellow, and red for contrast in the stars.

- ¾ yard light blue for A and B
- ¾ yard yellow for A and B
- ½ yard medium blue for A
- ½ yard red for A

Working with ticking is so much fun because it is irregularly striped and colors are bright. However--it tends to be stretchy. You can deal with the stretch by marking the templates on the straight of grain to cut out. This will minimize any stretching. Handle carefully and pin profusely. You can also make freezer paper templates that will stabilize the pattern pieces as you sew the blocks together. Just peel away when the blocks are completed.

Cutting and sewing

- Cut out templates for stars A, small triangles B and background shape C.
- C background is reversed for each side of star.

- Cut stars and triangle B on length and crossgrain for variety of pattern.
- Align right-angle corner of C on grain of fabric. The length grain is less stretchy than the crossgrain so lay out pattern with the arrow on the length of grain. This will give stability to the outside edge of the quilt.
- Cut (4) each of red, yellow, med blue and light blue A.
- Cut (2) and reverse (2) each of navy blue and cut (4) and reverse (4) of royal blue C.
- Cut (8) each yellow and light blue B.
- Piece four sections of blocks beginning with the star and small triangle.
- Piece C to one side of star and sew reverse C to other side.
- Piece the other three sections together in the same way.
- Sew the four sections as a four patch.
- Quilt and bind.

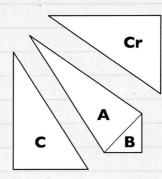

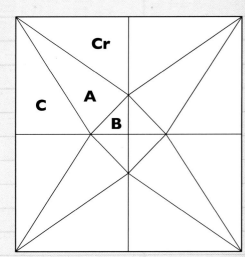

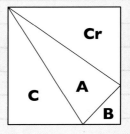

Rocky Road to Kansas
B

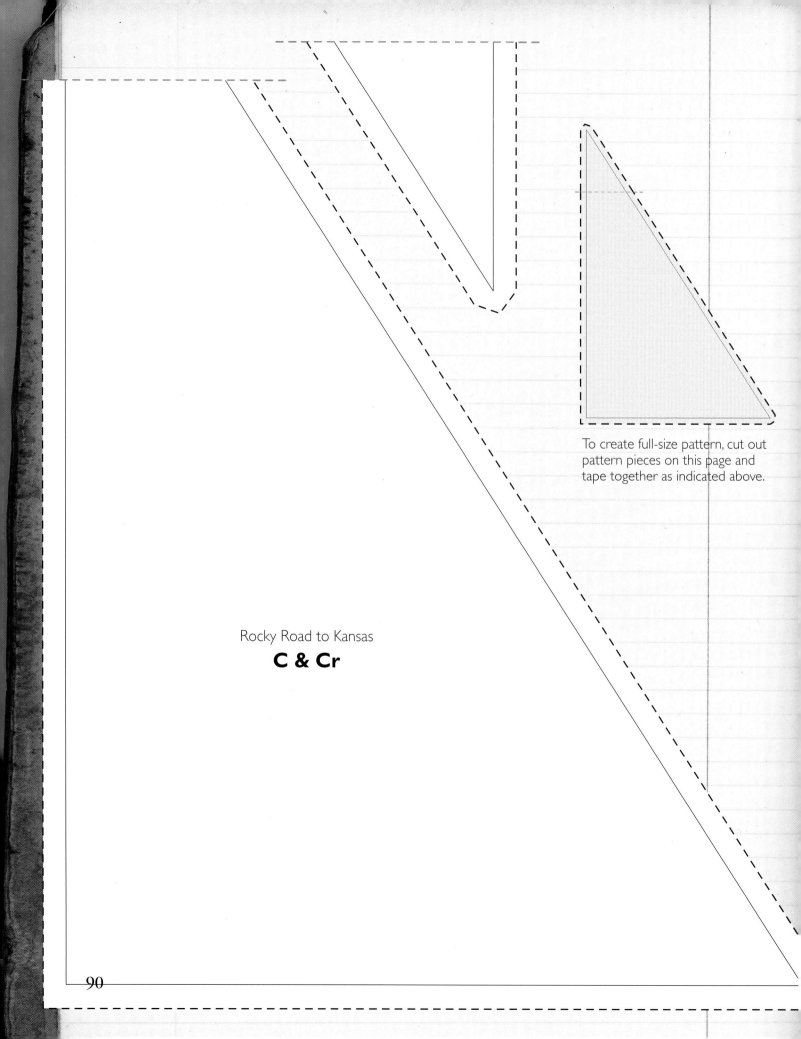

Rocky Road to Kansas
C & Cr

To create full-size pattern, cut out pattern pieces on this page and tape together as indicated above.

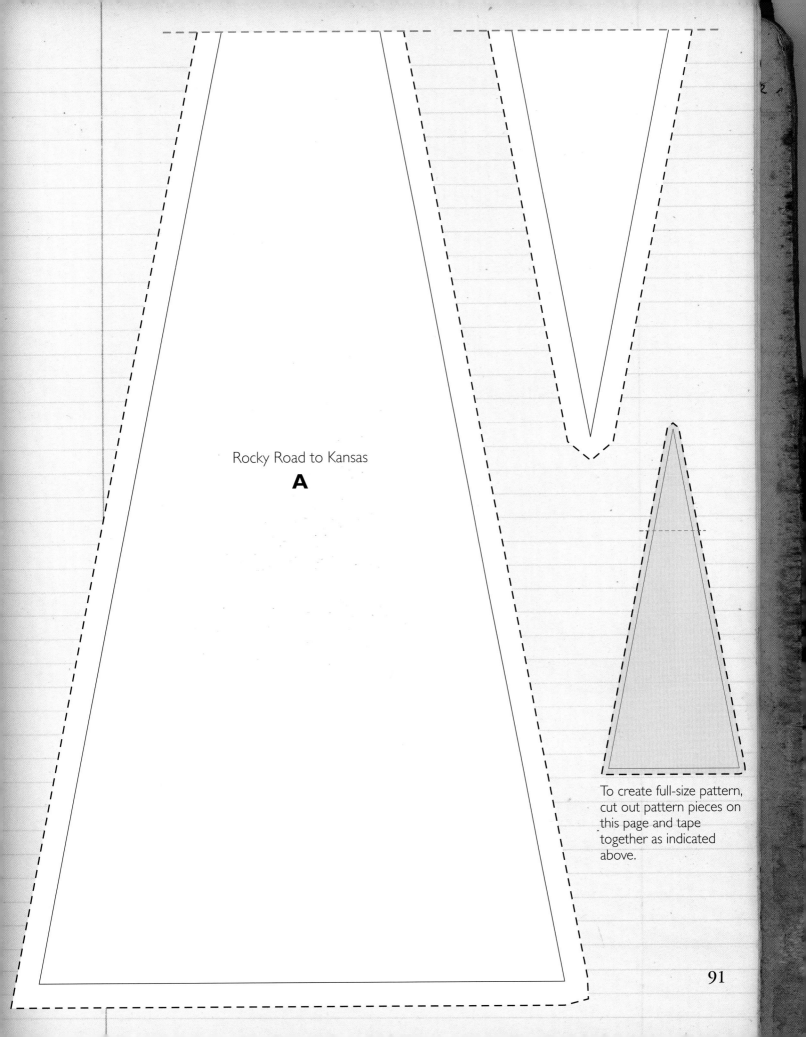

Rocky Road to Kansas
A

To create full-size pattern, cut out pattern pieces on this page and tape together as indicated above.

Hole in the Barn Door Pillowslip

21" x 36"

I enjoy using old quilt blocks for decorative projects that won't be quilted, washed or handled excessively. These charming vintage c.1880 "Hole in the Barn Door" blocks, sewn side by side together are the perfect size for a pillowcase for a guest bed. Use reproduction fabric--such as shirtings--for the background and printed calicos for the "Hole in the Barn Door". If you have a set of small 6"-8" old blocks, you could use them instead.

Yardage:

- 1 yard of shirting
- 8-9 fat quarters of dark or medium calico prints
- 1 yard woven stripe for back of pillow case
- ½ yard of a woven check for strips around blocks
- 1 yard muslin for lining behind patchwork

Sewing:

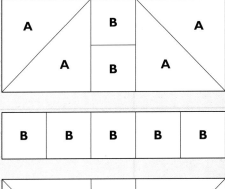

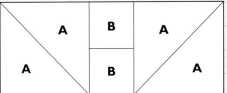

- Piece blocks as you would a nine-patch block.
- Set five blocks per row, then sew the strips into three rows, side by side. My old blocks are not all perfect so some points were cut off or blunted but I want the look of imperfection, a "made by candlelight in a sod house" look.
- Gently press finished blocks. Cut a piece of muslin bigger than set blocks. Lay underneath the set and baste together around edges. This serves as a good foundation for the pieced blocks and gives stability to the blocks.

Borders:

- Cut four 3 ½" strips on the crossgrain of woven check from bias to fold.
- Sew a strip to the top and bottom of pillowslip, then sew a strip to both sides.
- Fold strips back and gently press.
- Cut a backing a little larger than the finished top. Lay backing and top right sides together and pin.
- Begin sewing in top right corner and sew around leaving the top edge open. Turn inside out.
- On open edge of top border and backing, turn under ¼" twice and sew a hem.
- Fold top border in half and stitch around top border and backing by hand or machine.

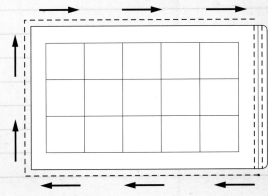

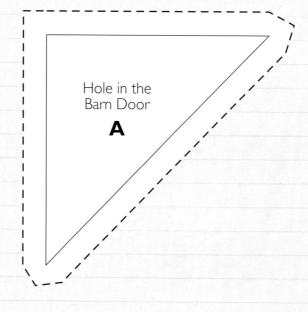

Hole in the
Barn Door

A

Hole in the
Barn Door

B

Redwork Splasher

"Let's Get Cleaned Up"

18" x 25"

Redwork splashers occupied the hands of many little girls and served as a "learn to embroider" piece for their hope chests. The splashers hung on the crossbar of a small two-drawer bedroom chest called a wash stand, upon which often sat a bowl and water pitcher. As people "washed up", the splasher prevented soapy water from splashing on the wallpaper behind the wash stand.

Supplies

- ½ yard white cotton muslin
- 1-2 skeins of DMC red embroidery floss
- embroidery hoop
- embroidery needle

Directions

- Cut muslin 18 ½" x 25 ½". Turn under a ¼" hem twice, stitch.
- Make a copy of the pattern sections and tape together.
- Place pattern on a light table. A storm window propped between two chairs with a lamp on the floor makes a good temporary light box.
- Trace pattern on the muslin with a #2 pencil.
- Use an outline stitch to stitch the pattern.
- Frame or hang on a splasher rod above the sink or on an antique bedroom wash stand.

To create full-size pattern, tape together this page with the following 3 pages as indicated above.

CLEANED UP.

America, Homeland of Patchwork Quilts

Heitzman family tending their berry patch in Texas. Photo from the collection of Terry Thompson.

America, Homeland of Patchwork Quilts

In the nineteenth century, immigrants from Europe left their homelands and sailed to the United States looking for land, opportunity, and freedom from oppressive living conditions. Germans, Swedes, Danish, Russians, and Dutch immigrants established settlements in Nebraska, Minnesota, Wisconsin, Iowa, and Kansas.

It was not unusual for husbands and fathers to go to America alone to find jobs, and then send for their wives and children. Many women faced the ocean voyage alone with their children and what they could manage to carry, leaving their parents and neighbors, with promises to write letters.

Not speaking English made the most simple tasks difficult, like asking for directions, finding the necessities of living such as food and water; and finding loved ones who had sent for them. Scoundrels often took advantage of immigrants and tricked them out of their money.

Somehow they found their way west to prairie homes in the Midwest where the promise of fertile, virgin soil and 160 acres of free land gave them hope for the future.

Ida Lindgren came to America from Sweden, and she and her husband settled on the tallgrass Konza Prairie in the Flint Hills close to Manhattan, Kansas. In her letters to her family in Sweden, she admits she complains a lot, but the letters also reveal her sense of humor. She mentions in one letter that "they had two Indians visiting, they were begging for food and money and Ida says that she wanted to beg too. They were wearing necklaces of very large beads and she would have liked to have one. When one of them said he wanted a piece of pork, she said he could have it if he gave her the necklace. He wouldn't give up the necklace but she gave him the pork anyway.

Ida worked as a dressmaker, sewing for herself and the neighboring women. She was exposed to her friends' and neighbors' sewing skills and their quilts. She mentions in a letter home that America seems to be the homeland of patchwork quilts. In a letter to her mother on November 20, 1870, she said:

"I am now back in Manhattan and sewing. I have been here about eight days and don't know when I will be going home. I am now getting one dollar a day and it is good to be earning something, so I will stay here as long as they want me and I will surely stay over my birthday. It will feel both empty and strange to sit among strangers that whole day and sew; surely more than one tear will fall on my work at the thought of bygone times, of other birthdays, when I had you with me. Oh well, how things have changed. I can rightly say, "tempora mutantur."

Mrs. John Verhoff recalled stories her grandfather often told of the forty-day voyage from Holland to Baltimore, Maryland, and settling into life in a new land. Unable to speak English and make a shopkeeper understand he wanted to buy "Ags," he resorted to cackling like a hen and then the storekeeper understood and brought him some eggs.

Another story from Mrs. Verhoff is about her son, Oliver. "In hard times, boxes of clothing and food were sent by Easterners to their Kansas relatives. I found a small red knitted hat that fit Oliver, wrapped him in quilts against the cold night. It was too much covering, and he sweated, the red hood faded, dying his hair deep red. I washed and washed but it never would come out. Sometime later we cut his hair, which was still red and which he disliked very much to have cut. For a year he was a red headed boy from the dye in that hood."

Another Swedish immigrant, Mrs. Swan Loftstead, tells of arriving by train to western Kansas on June 10, 1881, with "four children and $5.00 just 3 weeks after sailing from Sweden." When they got off the train, they were so thirsty she thought "How thankful I'd be if only I could ask for a drink of water in the American language."

The Loftstead family stayed with friends and ate their first meal "cooked on a stove heated with cow chips. I thought I would never be able to eat supper cooked with such a fuel, although I was very hungry. But we were so happy to be with old friends from our own country that I soon forgot the cow chips and relished the beautiful meal. During the years that followed I felt fortunate when there was an abundance of cow chips for us to stack up for winter fuel."

Weather was extreme at times and could change from bad to worse in a matter of minutes. Mrs. Loftstead tells of being caught in a blizzard, separated from her husband and their children left alone in their home. A neighbor tried to lead her horse-drawn sleigh back to her homestead but they became disoriented, abandoned the sleigh and walked to shelter. She could only think of her 9-month-old baby, who was being cared for by her 8-year-old girl Bessie. The hungry baby fussed and cried all night.

Meanwhile her husband, Swan, reached their homestead and found their house "covered with snow and it was so dark inside

Thomas B. Harryman and family, Long Creek, Grant Co, Oregon. Photo from the collection of Terry Thompson.

that the children thought it was still night. He fed the baby some warm coffee, bread, and milk. Then he warmed a quilt by the fire, wrapped the baby in it, and laid it in the cradle where the exhausted child went to sleep immediately. Then the men went to dig the horse out of the stable." Bessie called out the door, "Papa, it's smoking in here" and he called back, "Keep still, it'll soon be alright." She called to him three times when she screamed, "We are dying from the smoke." That brought Mr. Loftstead running. He found the room dense with smoke and one end of the cradle half burned. In warming the quilt for the baby, he had caught the quilt on fire. The baby was still asleep. We did not have a cradle for the baby anymore."

European women brought their old-world common sense and needlework skills with them as they settled into a new way of life in America—along with helpful hardiness, stubbornness, and a never-give-up attitude.

—Many of these stories were gathered by Mildren Cass Beason for her column "Pioneer Reminiscences" which appeared in weekly newspapers in Gove, Quinter, Grainfield and WaKeeney from 1937 to 1941.

"Every year there were prairie fires, most of them set by the railroad trains. We always kept a well-plowed fireguard around the buildings and sometimes a field. The dry years were the worst ones for fire, as the grass caught so easily. One night the whole family got out and fought a prairie fire all night long."

—Mrs. Swan Lofstead, 1881

"I don't have to work half as much here in Kansas (compared to Michigan). Some like it here, some don't. Here in America are many wanderers. I like it in Kansas but if I can get a good price I will sell and move to a better climate. America is very big. Very big! The Americans say, "You must get rich from speculation," and some I know became millionaires from speculation."

—Fabian Heitzman, January 1883

Fabian Heitzman and his wife's wedding portrait.
Photo from the collection of Terry Thompson.

Crazy quilts were quite the vogue from 1880-1920, made from silks, velvets, wools, rayons and more. Note the spools of thread on the table beside this stitcher. Photo from the collection of Terry Thompson.

"My parents told of happy times in Holland, attending skating parties on the Zuyder Zee in the winter time, of small houses on the ice where they could buy coffee and doughnuts on cold nights."

"I worked in a restaurant owned by an elderly couple from Holland, but I was too liberal with the food. Cowboys who came in off the range, not having home cooking for some time always had ferocious appetites, and I served all anyone wanted to eat. When my first baby was born, ladies of the town wondered if I had clothes for the baby. I bought materials and made nice baby clothes. They were all surprised to see such a nice layette."

—Mrs. John Verhoff

"One night Oliver was tossing a ball, stepped backward and a small rattlesnake bit him. The children hurried home and I bathed his foot well in Indigo bluing water, then his father dug a hole in the mud and had Oliver stick his foot down in the mud. His foot swelled to the knee and turned bluish green, but before long he recovered. When Oliver was 11 years old, he earned money herding sheep, at age 12 he bought a gun and kept the family supplied with fresh meat, duck, deer, and rabbits. They shot so many ducks, restaurants in Chicago paid them $3.00 per dozen shipped."

—Mrs. John Verhoff

107

Homespun

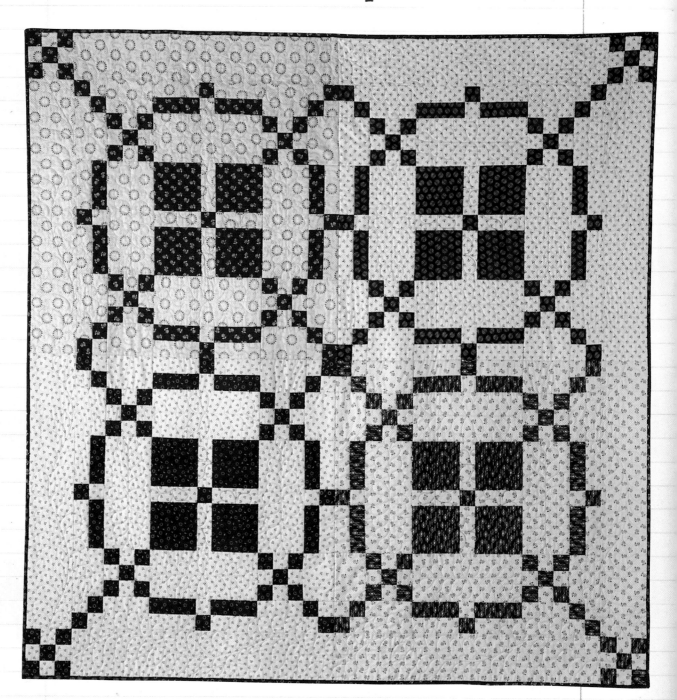

"America is very big. Very big!"

Size: 72" x 72"

The design similarities between 19th century four block quilts and woven coverlets led me to create a quilt that looks homespun and woven. I saw a picture of a Pennsylvania quilt c. 1875 made of nine patch squares and rectangles and thought it would adapt nicely to the four block format.

Indigo blue and white wool overshot and woven coverlets were the most common colors so I chose blue and white cotton prints to recreate the coverlet look in a quilt.

The patterns are so simple to rotary cut and sew, and the end result looks like an old vintage coverlet. Make four blocks, then sew them together and you are done. If you wish to add borders to make the quilt larger, please do. However, I liked the simplicity of just the four blocks. Begin with a sharp rotary blade as every pattern piece is rotary cut. There are no templates for this quilt.

Yardage

- 1½ yards of four different indigo blue prints
- 1 yard of four different ecru or white prints
- Rotary cutting tool, blades, mat, accurate ruler

If you prefer to use only 1 blue and I white fabric, you need:

- 6 yards indigo blue print
- 4 yards white or ecru print

Cutting and sewing

- Pre-wash fabric to release the overdye on the indigo fabric.
- Follow the cutting guide for a one block or four block.

To make one block, cut:

A: 2¼" x 2¼": 38 dark, 32 light

B: 5⅞" x 4⅛": 8 light

C: 5⅞" x 2¼": 12 light, 8 dark

D: 31⅛" x 5⅞": 2 light

E: 13⅛" x 5⅞": 4 light

F: 5⅞" x 5⅞": 4 dark

To make four blocks, cut:

A: 2¼" x 2¼": 152 dark, 128 light

B: 5⅞" x 4⅛": 32 light

C: 5⅞" x 2¼": 48 light, 32 dark

D: 31⅛" x 5⅞": 8 light

E: 13⅛" x 5⅞": 16 light

F: 5⅞" x 5⅞": 16 dark

Stitch:

- Piece each block in the same fashion.
- Piece each block as you would piece a large nine patch. Break the pattern down into five rows.

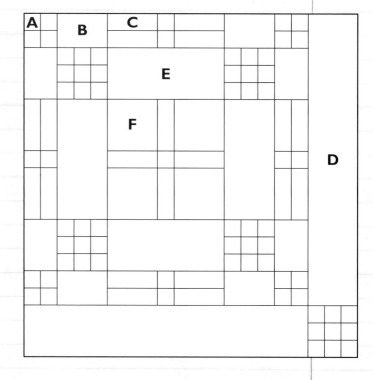

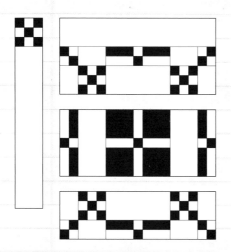

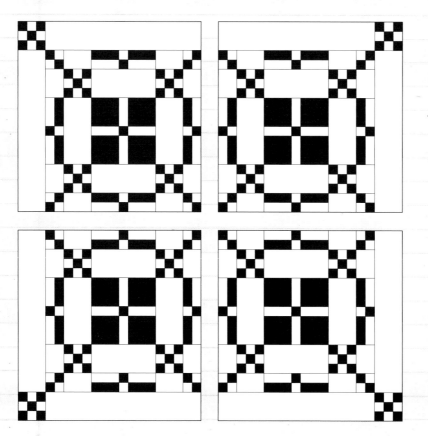

- Set pieced blocks side by side referring to the drawn chart. Each corner has a nine-patch block in it.

Our homespun quilt is quilted with feathered vines throughout.

Cotton Crazies

Size: 18" x 27"

The late 19th century craze for making crazy quilts included cotton-made quilts as well as the luxury fabrics of silk, velvet and wool. Not many of them have survived, probably because they were used and washed instead of being draped over fainting couches in Victorian parlors. The few I have seen were appliquéd to muslin or printed calico foundation squares. Unlike their silken sisters, there is no embroidery covering the appliquéd seams.

I like the crazy quilt look but have not really wanted to collect fancy fabrics or do the elaborate embroidery work. These cotton crazies look rather primitive and homey, something our rural grandmothers would have made with their leftover dressmaking scraps.

Directions for making a small crazy quilt:

- Cut 6, 9½" muslin or calico squares for foundations.
- Assemble scraps of light, medium and dark cotton, or cut squares, triangles or rectangles of different lengths and widths.
- Lay out contrasting colors, beginning in one corner and cover block with scraps, overlapping shapes, pinning as you go. When you are satisfied with the block, tuck under seam allowance of shapes and appliqué. Repeat process for all blocks. Sew finished blocks into two rows of three blocks. Sew on a backing or quilt.

Unknown woman, circa 1890. She has the determined look of so many pioneer women. Photo from the collection of Terry Thompson.

Mary Jane Scruggs
Exoduster

Inscription on back reads Mae Belle Brown, May 1880. Photo from the collection of Terry Thompson.

26

All Colored People

THAT WANT TO

GO TO KANSAS,

On September 5th, 1877,

Can do so for $5.00

IMMIGRATION.

WHEREAS, We, the colored people of Lexington, Ky., knowing that there is an abundance of choice lands now belonging to the Government, have assembled ourselves together for the purpose of locating on said lands. Therefore,

BE IT RESOLVED, That we do now organize ourselves into a Colony, as follows:— Any person wishing to become a member of this Colony can do so by paying the sum of one dollar ($1.00), and this money is to be paid by the first of September, 1877, in instalments of twenty-five cents at a time, or otherwise as may be desired.

RESOLVED, That this Colony has agreed to consolidate itself with the Nicodemus Towns, Solomon Valley, Graham County, Kansas, and can only do so by entering the vacant lands now in their midst, which costs $5.00.

RESOLVED, That this Colony shall consist of seven officers—President, Vice-President, Secretary, Treasurer, and three Trustees. President—M. M. Bell; Vice-President —Isaac Talbott; Secretary—W. J. Niles; Treasurer—Daniel Clarke; Trustees—Jerry Lee, William Jones, and Abner Webster.

RESOLVED, That this Colony shall have from one to two hundred militia, more or less, as the case may require, to keep peace and order, and any member failing to pay in his dues, as aforesaid, or failing to comply with the above rules in any particular, will not be recognized or protected by the Colony.

114

B. Singelton & A. McClure
Imagration.

Mary Jane Scruggs
Exoduster

A bold red and green appliqué quilt top appeared at Kansas Quilt Project Discovery Days in Stockton in 1987. It was passed down through the Scruggs family of Nicodemus, Kansas, with the familiar situation of "maker unknown." It could have been made by Mary Jane Lewis Scruggs, the daughter of ex-slaves from Kentucky, or by her mother, Amanda Lewis, or perhaps even by someone outside the family.

What is known is that the Scruggs family was part of a movement of African-Americans who left the South in the late 1870s following the Civil War to settle in western states. This exodus reached its peak in 1879-1880, as thousands of blacks, apprehensive over the possible reinstitution of slavery, migrated west toward the "promised land" of Kansas. They became known as "Exodusters." It was the most notable migration of southern blacks in the second half of the nineteenth century.

Early Exodusters came to Graham County's South Solomon River Valley to Nicodemus, which was established in 1877. The initial Nicodemus settlers were former slaves from north of Lexington, Kentucky, who had left the South in search of independence and better opportunities in the high plains Kansas.

Many risked their last cash to buy a railroad ticket to go west, where they had been assured of "game in abundance, wild horses free for the taming, and marvelously fertile land."

What they found was hardly that.

"When we came in sight the men shouted, 'There is Nicodemus …' I looked with all the eyes I had but could see no town. 'Where is Nicodemus? I don't see it.' Then my husband pointed to various smokes coming out of the ground and said, 'See, that is Nicodemus…' The people lived in dugouts. We again put up tents. The scenery to me was not inviting and I began to cry."

— *Biography of Mrs. Willina Lewis Hickman*

Mary Jane Scruggs was not part of that first wave of settlers, but her future husband was. Robert B. "Grave" Scruggs came from Georgetown in Scott County, Kentucky (north of Lexington). He came in 1878, seeing his "chance to own a real piece of land," and married Mary Jane Lewis in 1889. Mary Jane was born Feb. 5, 1866, in Richmond, Missouri. Her family moved near Concordia in Cloud County in 1881. Robert and Mary Jane first lived near Bogue, a small community five miles southwest of Nicodemus. They had two daughters, Alva, born in 1890, and Ola, born in 1892. Later they moved near Nicodemus, where they owned 720 acres of land at the time of her death in 1934. Shortly after that, Scruggs divided part of his land between his two daughters. "We was just so proud of th' land!" he said.

Their land became part of an annual Nicodemus celebration. The annual Nicodemus picnic held August 1 to celebrate Emancipation Day was long held in Scruggs' Grove. A large carnival usually was set up in the grove for a three-day affair (one day before to warm up and one day after to recover). Basket dinners, food concessions, political speaking, baseball, and dancing completed the attractions.

Early years of the colony were characterized by extreme poverty. Many of the settlers moved on. But growth was constant. By 1887, the town had 150 inhabitants and a number of business and services. In 1888 the proposed extension of the railroad through Nicodemus fueled an influx of settlers, but the tracks were laid six miles southwest of town. The town reached a peak population of 595 in 1910. Like surrounding towns, it lost inhabitants in the Great Depression.

Original pomegranate quilt, possibly made by Mary Jane Scruggs or her mother Amanda Lewis. Photo courtesy of Kansas State Historical Society.

Nicodemus Rose

"We was just so proud of th' land"

52" x 52"

This is an adaptation of the stunning quilt Valaria Thomas brought to Quilt Discovery Day in 1987, with a simplified pomegranate appliqué pattern. I also chose to make just one block, place it on point, square it up with corner triangles, and change the common name to Nicodemus Rose. May you think of those many hopeful former slaves who came to Kansas as you make this quilt. The original quilt was donated to the Kansas State Historical Society.

Materials/yardage

- 2" Clover bias maker
- 1 ⅛ yard dark blue print for the 36 1/2" block
- 1 ⅝ yard of light blue for corner triangles
- 1 yard of striped print for bias stems (cut 2" wide)
- 1 ¼ yard red for roses, star, diamonds, small center circle
- Four fat quarters of gold/yellow for leaves and diamonds
- ¾ yard of white dots for rose petals and large rose
- Scrap of black for center circle of star
- 1 yard stripe for binding

Cutting

Block and corner triangles

- Cut out background block 36 ½" (seam allowance is included)
- Fold on diagonal (fig 1) and gently press a line from corner to corner to use as a guideline for placing center vine (fig 2). You are pressing on the bias so be careful not to stretch the block.
- For corner triangles cut two 25 ⅛" squares. Cut them on the diagonal (fig 3) to make four corner triangles.

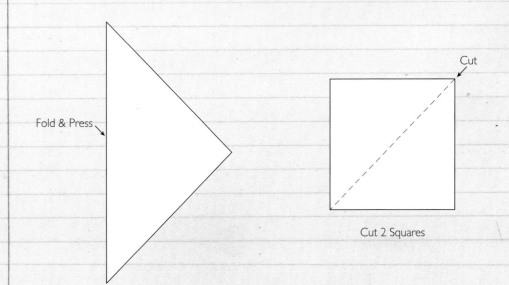

Fold & Press

Cut

Cut 2 Squares

Bias strips
- Cut 2" width of long bias strips for center stems and side stems.
- Pull 2" bias fabric strips thru the 1" bias maker. Loosely wrap bias strips around a cardboard to keep the folds in place until sewn.

Roses, leaves, diamonds for 36" square and corner triangles—cut:
- 19 red roses A, 19 white petals B
- 45 yellow leaves D
- 7 yellow diamonds E
- 14 red diamonds E
- 1 white large star C
- 1 red small star H
- 1 black large circle F
- 1 red small circle G

Sewing

Bias stem layout
- Lay out creased background block on table.
- Lay prepared 1" long bias strips down center fold line. Everything will connect to this center strip. Pin in place.
- Lay out, by sight, the two cross stems (21" long) and 14" from the bottom point. Layout (2) curved 11" stem, 16 ½" above the first bias stem.
- Pin all stems in place.

Roses and petals
- Prepare appliqué units for hand or machine appliqué.
- Place prepared rose units, leaves, and diamonds, referring to quilt photograph. Pin in place.
- Place square on design wall and if all designs look in place, baste stems, roses and leaves.
- Appliqué all designs.

Corner triangles

- Place stems from the corner and out to the sides, referring to picture. Center stems measure 13" and side stems are 16".
- Place roses and leaves. Pin and baste. Appliqué.
- Sew finished triangles to side of center block.
- Block will float ¼" to ½" above the squares corners.
- Quilt and bind.

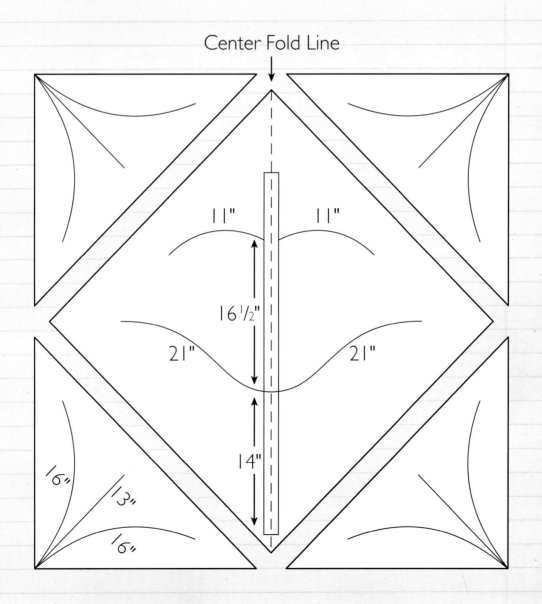

Center Fold Line

11"   11"

16½"

21"   21"

14"

16"

13"

16"

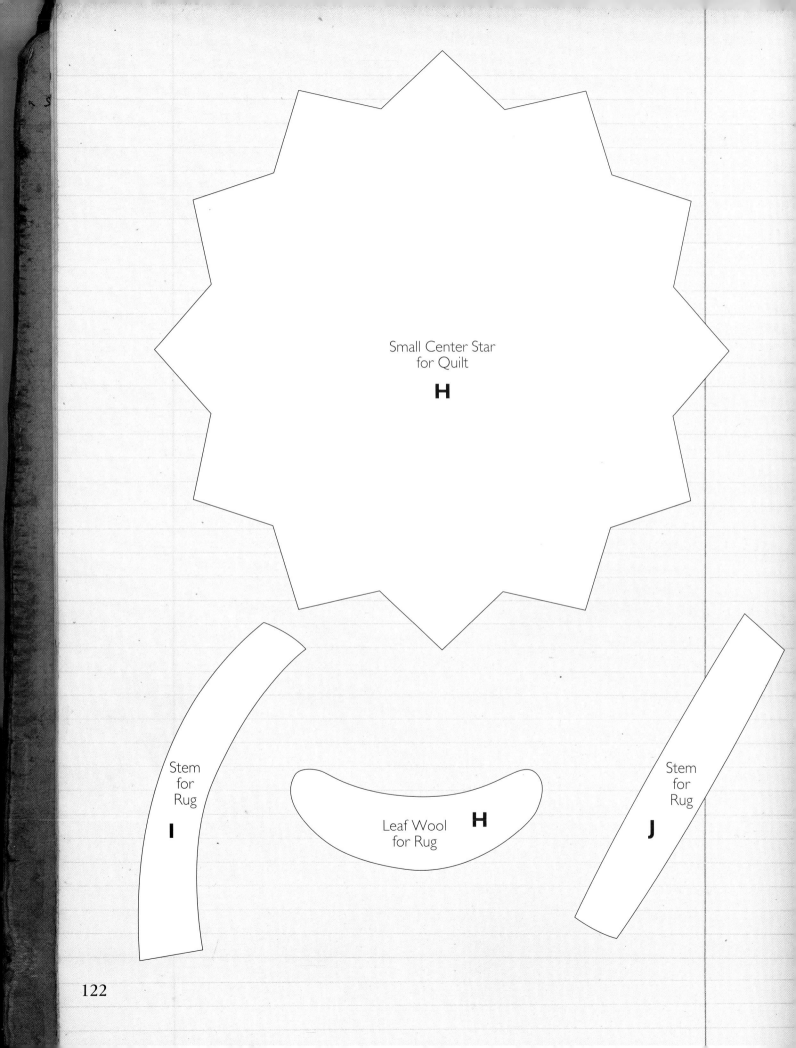

Small Center Star
for Quilt

H

Stem
for
Rug

I

Leaf Wool
for Rug

H

Stem
for
Rug

J

122

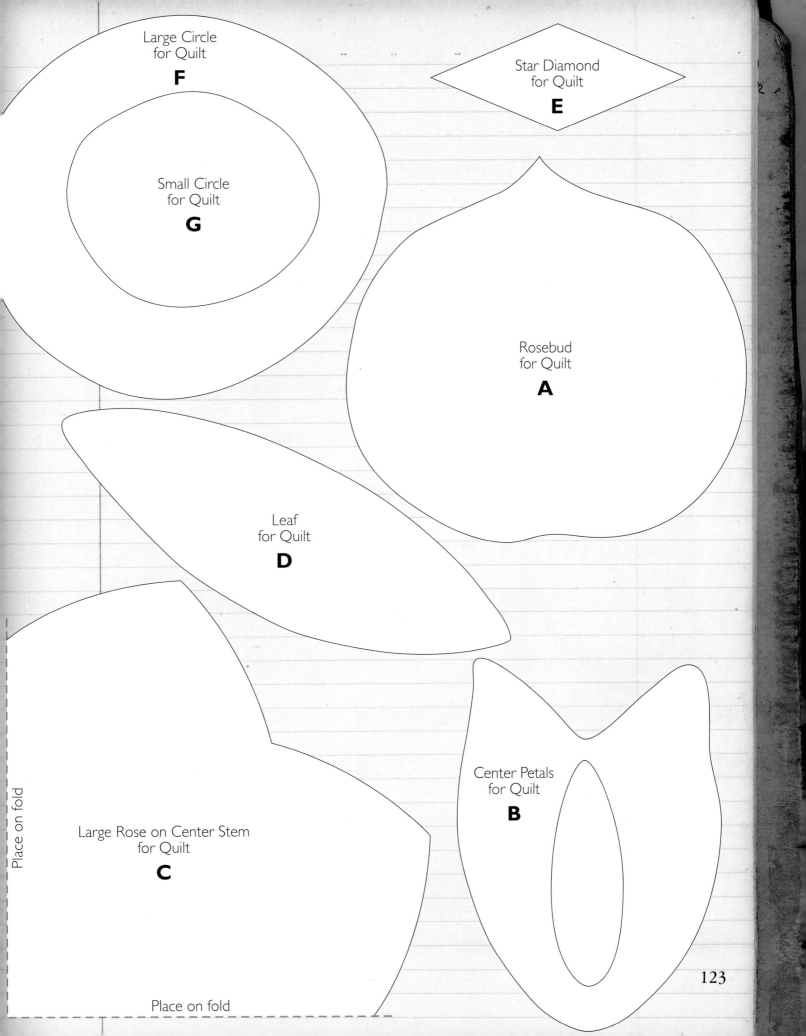

Large Circle
for Quilt

F

Small Circle
for Quilt

G

Star Diamond
for Quilt

E

Rosebud
for Quilt

A

Leaf
for Quilt

D

Center Petals
for Quilt

B

Place on fold

Large Rose on Center Stem
for Quilt

C

Place on fold

123

A Crock of Flowers

16" x 16"

I appreciate the virtues of working with wool for appliquéing small table rugs, pillows and small wall quilts. Cut a design and don't worry about the edges raveling. The needle slides easily as you sew and the buttonhole stitch adds an embellished look around each appliqué. Simple shapes are perfect for wool appliqué and many quilt shops now have a section for wool supplies.

This little table rug is a variation of the Nicodemus Rose pattern with the wild prairie flowers and berries that greeted Mary Jane as she settled in her new home in Kansas.

Supplies

- 16" x 16" square of dark blue plaid wool for background.
- Small pieces of green for stems and leaves, red for flowers and dots. Add burnt orange, shaded ecru for the crock, gold, blue for berries.
- I used a variegated embroidery thread that looks like perle cotton.
- Freezer paper for templates.
- Large eye embroidery needle.

Directions

- Draw patterns on freezer paper.
- Press freezer paper patterns on the selected colors for every pattern piece. Let paper/wool cool.
- Cut out around freezer paper: no seam allowance is needed.
- Follow the picture for placement of crock and stems.
- Embroider with a buttonhole stitch.
- Place D on C and place inside center of B for large flower. Add calyx E under B.
- Place (4) Ds on G for blanket flower. Place both units at top of stems J.
- Place (5) Ds on left drooping stem I. Sew small circles to (3) trumpet vine F. Place flower on right drooping vine I.
- Place leaves H on stem and over trumpet vine.
- Embroider dots all around picture: 7 small and 7 large dots.
- Place in a picture frame or place on a special little table.

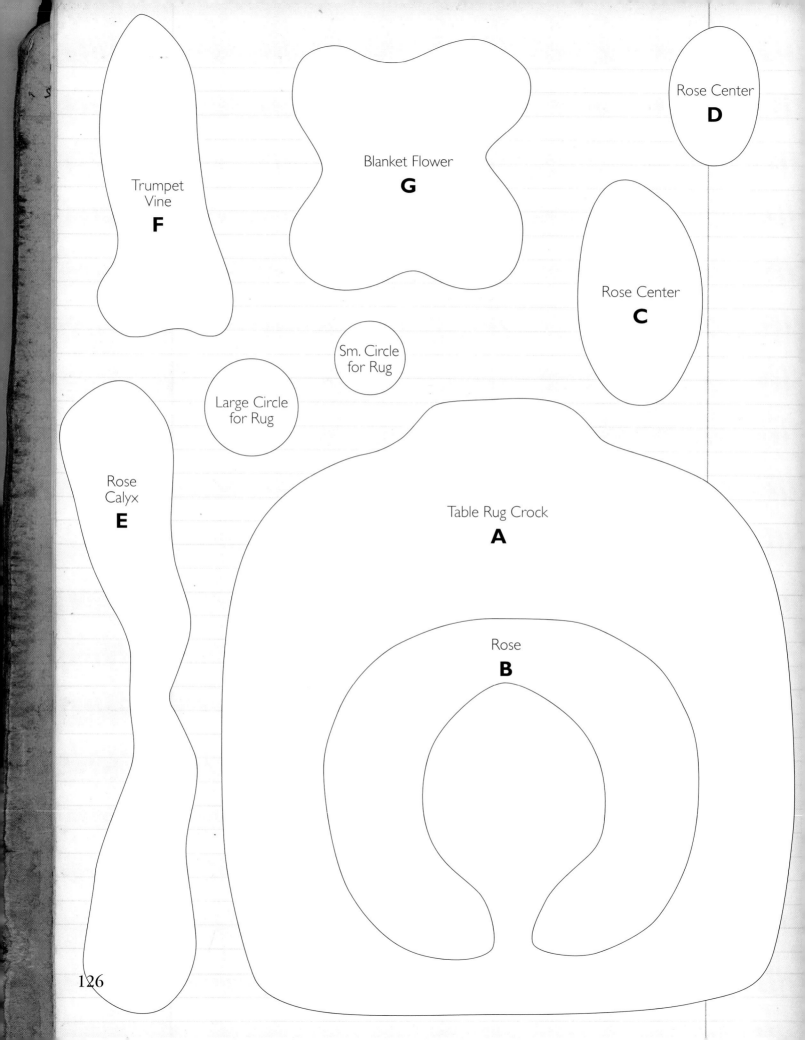

Rose Center
D

Trumpet
Vine
F

Blanket Flower
G

Rose Center
C

Sm. Circle
for Rug

Large Circle
for Rug

Rose
Calyx
E

Table Rug Crock
A

Rose
B

126

Mary Harris
and Bird Russ

Mary Harris, seated with family members.
Bird Russ is on the right. Photo from the
collection of Terry Thompson.

128

Unknown Native American mother and child. Note the pieced quilts in the background. Photo from the collection of Terry Thompson.

Mary Harris and Bird Russ
Mother and Daughter

Written family records are slim on Mary Harris' history — but family members believe they were former slaves. Mary's Cherokee name is lost, but it is thought she came from Oklahoma and at one time owned land that was later taken away from her by the government. In the 19th century it was not uncommon to enslave native Americans, and intermarriage between blacks and Indians was accepted.

It is also possible that Mary was sent to an Indian mission school where she learned sewing. In an effort to "civilize" Indian children, the government forced children to leave their parents and live at Indian mission schools run by white clergy. The girls learned cooking, sewing, and gardening.

Mary married Jacob Harris, and they settled in LaMonte, Missouri, where their only child, Bird Ella, was born on October 20, 1871.

Mary and Jacob were probably farmers who struggled to survive after the devastation of the Civil War. Former slaves faced the hardships of being legally free, but lived in an atmosphere of prejudice and resentment, making their lives more difficult.

At age 22, Bird Ella married Richard Orme, and the young couple raised four children. After her husband's death, Bird married Thomas Russ of Wichita, Kansas, where she probably lived close to her mother Mary. They later moved to Kansas City, Kansas.

Bird Russ or "Russie" as her grandchildren called her, stood six feet tall and had reddish black hair and the facial features of her Indian mother. Bird Ella learned needlework skills from her mother, Mary. She pieced a "Rising Sun" red and white quilt top around 1890, judging from the fabric and hand-sewing techniques. She and her mother may have worked together on this top and another red and white pieced Drunkard's path top, both handed down through the family as unquilted tops.

Bird's needlework skills filled her home with lovely embroidered sheets and towels and handmade quilts. She could look at a picture of clothing in a catalogue and reproduce it without using a pattern. Her skilled hands guided the small hands of her granddaughters as they sat in her lap learning to crochet. Her doilies and pillowcases trimmed with hand-crocheted lace remain in the memories of her family.

After her death at age 92, she was remembered in a letter to her family from her friend A. B. May.

"In 1934, Mrs. Russ moved into the neighborhood becoming my next door neighbor. We at once formed a friendship that lasted thru the years. She was kind, considerate and industrious with a religious nature. How well do we remember the beautiful vegetable and floral garden she cultivated. There were a variety of vegetables and flowers growing always which she loved to share. She found much pleasure in the out doors enjoying all the wonderful blessings of God, the free air, sunshine and even the rain. May God bless and keep you." Sorrowfully submitted, The Neighbors, Kansas City, Kansas, Feb. 22, 1963.

Chips and Whetstone

"She found much pleasure in the outdoors"

Size: 76" x 76"

When thinking about a pieced four block quilt to represent Mary and Bird, I chose the Chips and Whetstone pattern. I saw a quilt top pieced by Bird when I interviewed her granddaughters and the pattern was a variation of the Harvest Sun genre. Too difficult for me to piece (and others I suspect), I instead decided on a pattern that seemed more do-able. Karalee Fisher pieced this beautiful quilt. She said this pattern is not for beginners. So—decide where your piecing skills lie and go for it!

Yardage

½ yard each of three different blues for diamonds and border squares

⅝ yard each of two blues for corners of diamond blocks

½ yard each of three different rust/reddish browns for diamonds and border squares

⅝ yard each of two rust/reddish browns for corners of diamond blocks

2¾ yard of tan for circle wedges and border triangles around squares

Please read all directions before beginning.

Let's talk about color placement. To best show off the diamonds, I alternated tan and rust in the center of two blocks and placed light and dark blue diamonds on the outside edges of the blocks. For the other two blocks, I reversed the order. I placed blue and tan diamonds in the center and light and dark rusts on the outside edge of blocks. You can study this in the picture.

Chips and Whetstone - Diamond blocks (4)
Cutting for each block:

- Create a template for each pattern piece, mark 'long side' and 'short side' on piece B.
- Cut 8 dark (blue or rust) B
- Cut 8 light (blue or rust) B
- Cut 4 dark (blue or rust) A
- Cut 4 tan A
- Cut 8 tan C
- Cut 8 tan D
- Cut 4 (blue or rust) E. Be sure to place template on fold of fabric, using the fold line on pattern as a guide and to tape the top and bottom of template together.

132

Sewing

This is the easy part. If you piece in units this is a breeze. Refer to Figure 1.

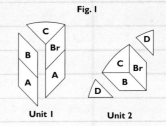

Fig. 1

Unit 1   Unit 2

- For each block, create (4) of Unit 1 and (4) of Unit 2. As you create the units — on any angle as in figure 1 — do not sew seams to the end of seam allowance. Stop stitching at the seam line. This leaves an opening for inserting pattern pieces C and D.
- Referring to Figure 2, assemble units into one diamond block, again, stop stitching at the seam line in order to set the next unit in with ease.
- After center circle is set and corner pattern pieces E have been cut, sew a ¼" stay stitch line around finished circle and the corner square to prevent stretching as you sew.
- Piece together the short ends of pieces E to create a square with an empty circle in the middle. See Figure 3. You then mark the center of the ¼ circle points on the fold lines with a pin. Fold the diamond block in half and mark with pins then fold in half again and mark the ¼ points with pins.
- Right sides together and matching stay stitch lines, match up the half circle pins on the pieced diamond block with the seam line on corner squares. Pin.
- Match up the ¼ points on the pieced diamond with the ¼ point (fold line) on the corner circle and pin. All curves are on the bias so gently handle circles with care to not stretch them. Pin all around circle and sew. See Figure 4.

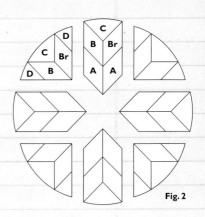

Fig. 2

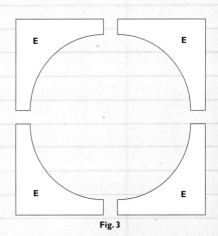

Fig. 3

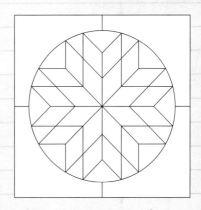

Fig. 4

Borders – 12 strips
Cutting

- Cut total of 48 blue 3 ⅜" squares C using your three shades of blue.
- Cut a total of 48 rust 3 ⅜" squares C using your three shades of rust.
- Cut 42 tan 5 ¼" squares, cut on both diagonals for 168 triangles B. Refer to Figure 5.
- Cut 24 tan 2⅞" squares, cut in half on the diagonal for 48 triangles A. See Figure 6.

Blocks to set strips – 9 blocks
Cutting

- Cut 5 blue 3⅜" squares C.
- Cut 4 rust 3⅜" squares C.
- Cut 10 rust 2⅞" squares, cut in half on the diagonal for 20 triangles A. See Figure 6.
- Cut 8 blue 2⅞" squares, cut in half on the diagonal for 16 triangles A. See Figure 6.

Sewing - for each strip

- Referring to Figure 7, piece one unit 1, one unit 3 and six of unit 2.
- Piece the six unit 2s together put unit 1 on one end and unit 3 on the other end.
- Attach one tan triangle A to each end of the border strip in order to square it off. See Figure 7.
- Repeat for all 12 strips.
- Follow Figure 8 to create 4 rust squares C with blue triangles A connecting blocks. Then create 5 blue squares C with rust triangles A connecting blocks.

Fig. 5

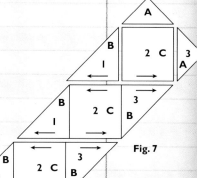

Fig. 6

Fig. 7

Fig. 8

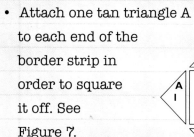

134

Setting Quilt

- Sew a border strip to the left and right sides of one diamond block. Sew the next diamond block to the unit and sew a border strip to the right side of the last diamond block to create row 1.
- Repeat for a row 2.
- Sew 2 units of the following to create the top and bottom borders: one rust block, a border strip, a blue block, a border strip and end with a rust block.
- Sew 1 unit of the following to create the center sash: one blue block, a border strip, a blue block, a border strip and end with a blue block.
- Sew the top border to the top of row 1.
- Sew the center sash to the bottom of row 1 and the top of row 2.
- Sew the bottom border to the bottom of row 2.
- Quilt and bind.

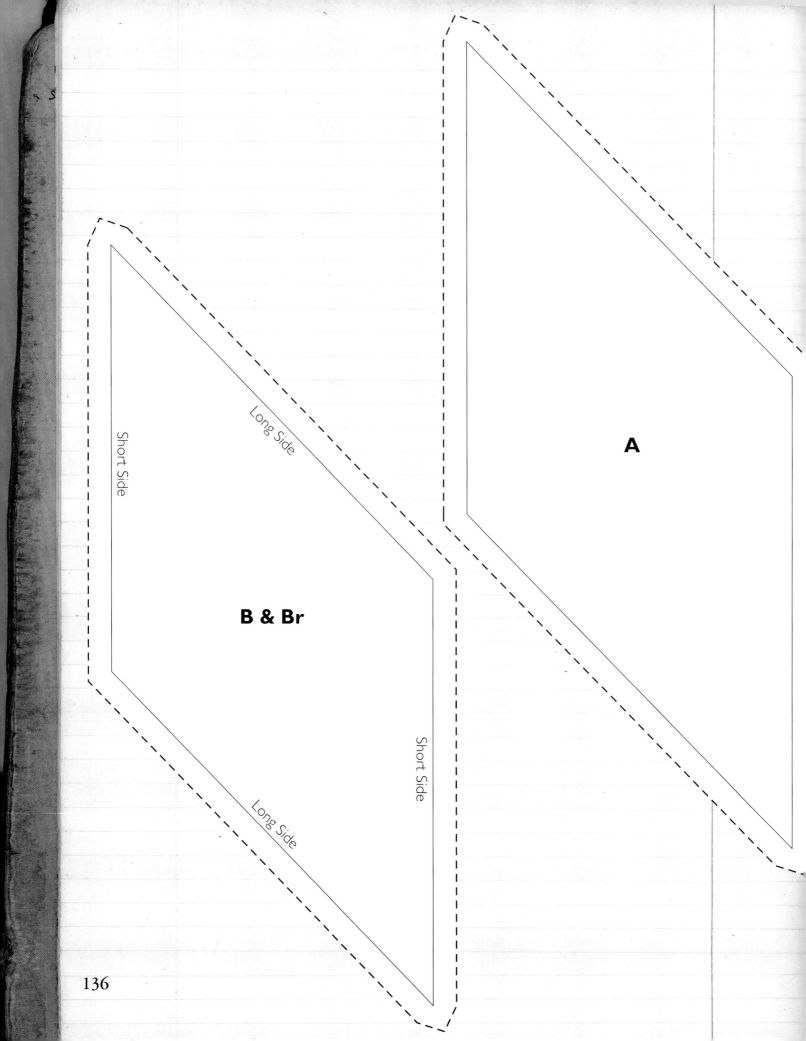

A

B & Br

Long Side

Short Side

Short Side

Long Side

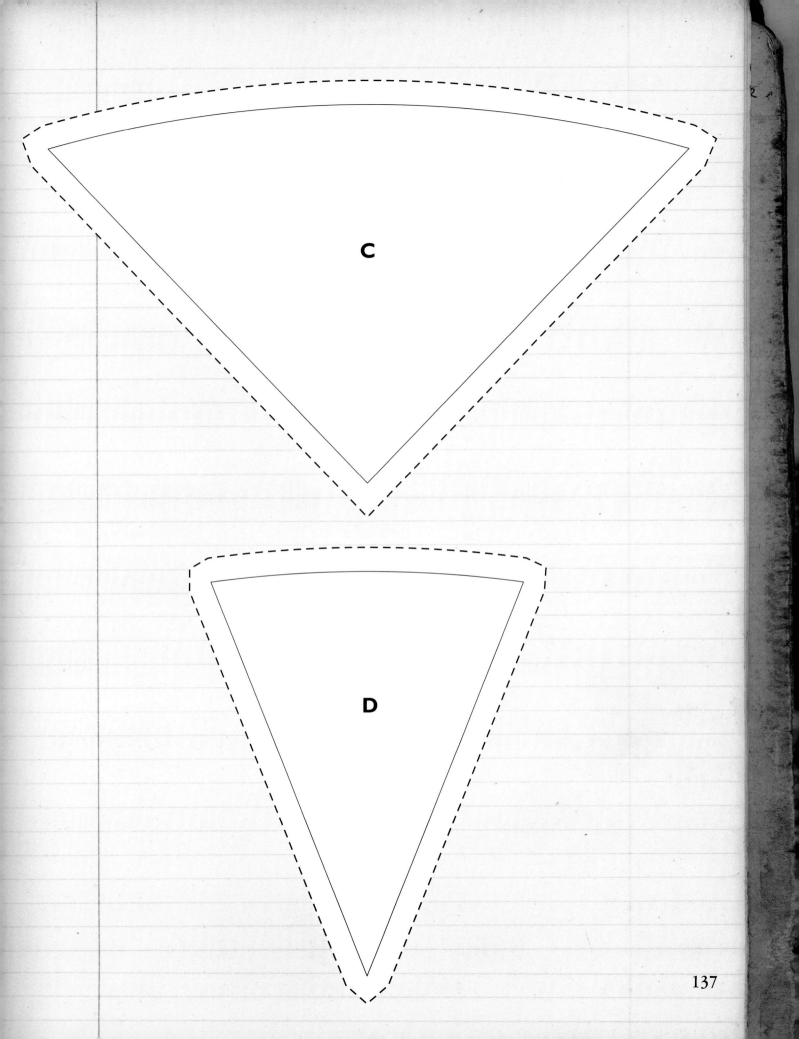

C

D

137

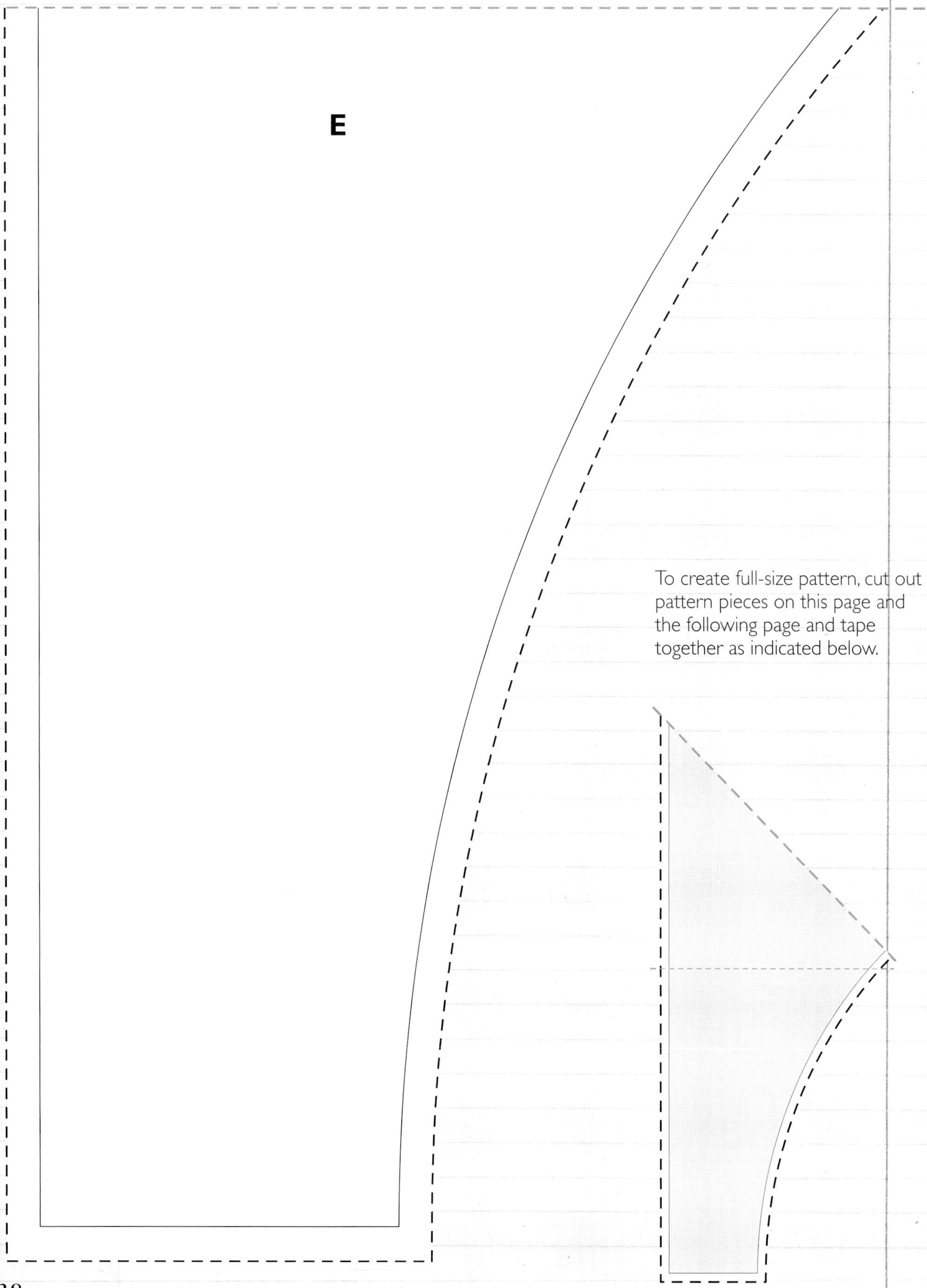

E

To create full-size pattern, cut out pattern pieces on this page and the following page and tape together as indicated below.

138

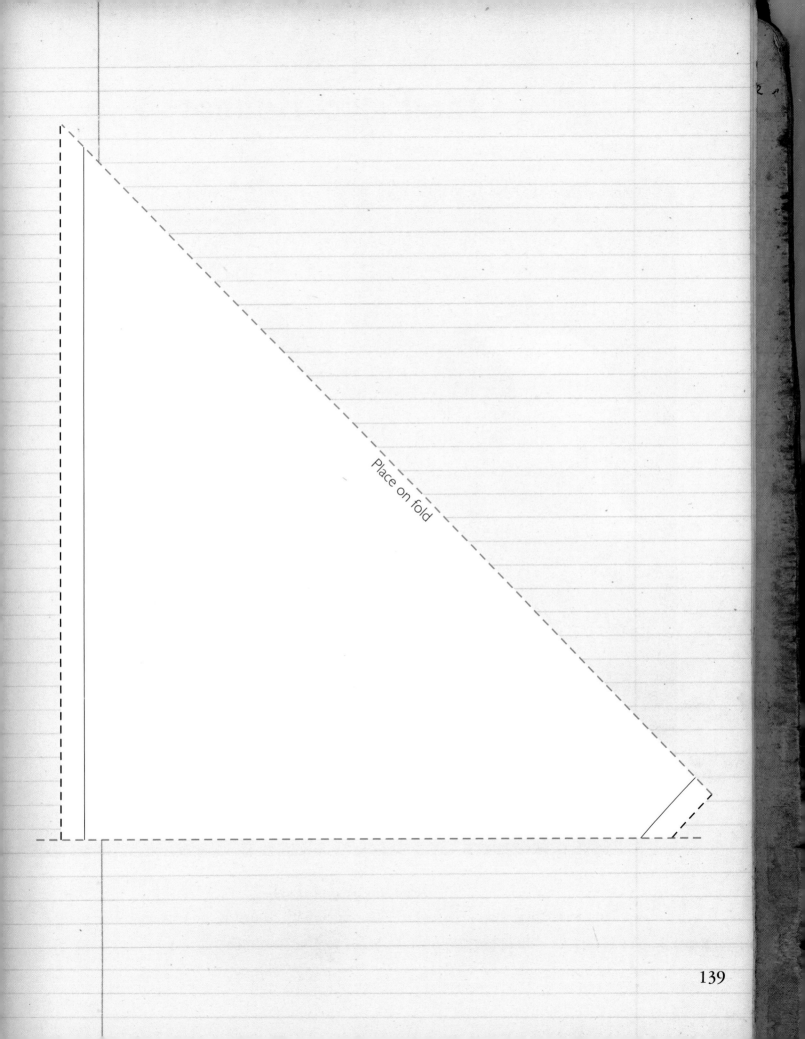

Place on fold

139

One-Piece Bonnet

Toddler or infant size

This is the most simple to make of all sunbonnets. There is one pattern piece, plus the tie pieces. It may be sewn quickly on the sewing machine.

Slat bonnets were designed to be worn on windy days. The cardboard slats keep the brim stiff and save the time of quilting the brim. They should be removed from their slots when washed and replaced when the bonnet is dry. You may want to number the slats so that they will return to the same slot, just in case the slots vary a little in size.

Materials

- ½ yard 45" cotton calico
- Thread
- Button

Instructions

- Pin bonnet pattern to folded fabric. Cut out, adding ¼" seams.
- Cut out two ties: 1½" x 36" (adjust length as desired).
- Turn under and sew bonnet raw edges under ⅛", then under again ¼": stitch. Do the same with ties.
- Mark one-inch slat lines on flap.
- Fold back slat flap to inside of bonnet. Pin around edges to keep from shifting. Slip end of ties inside flap and stitch over.
- Starting at left side of flap, sew down edge, then make a line of stitching where lines were marked. These lines create the slots for slats.
- Cut slats from poster board, just slightly smaller than slots so that fit will be snug, but still not break the seams.
- On back of bonnet, tack o's to o's and sew a button on to cover tacking.

Idea: use modern day milk jug plastic for slats. They wouldn't have to be removed for washing.

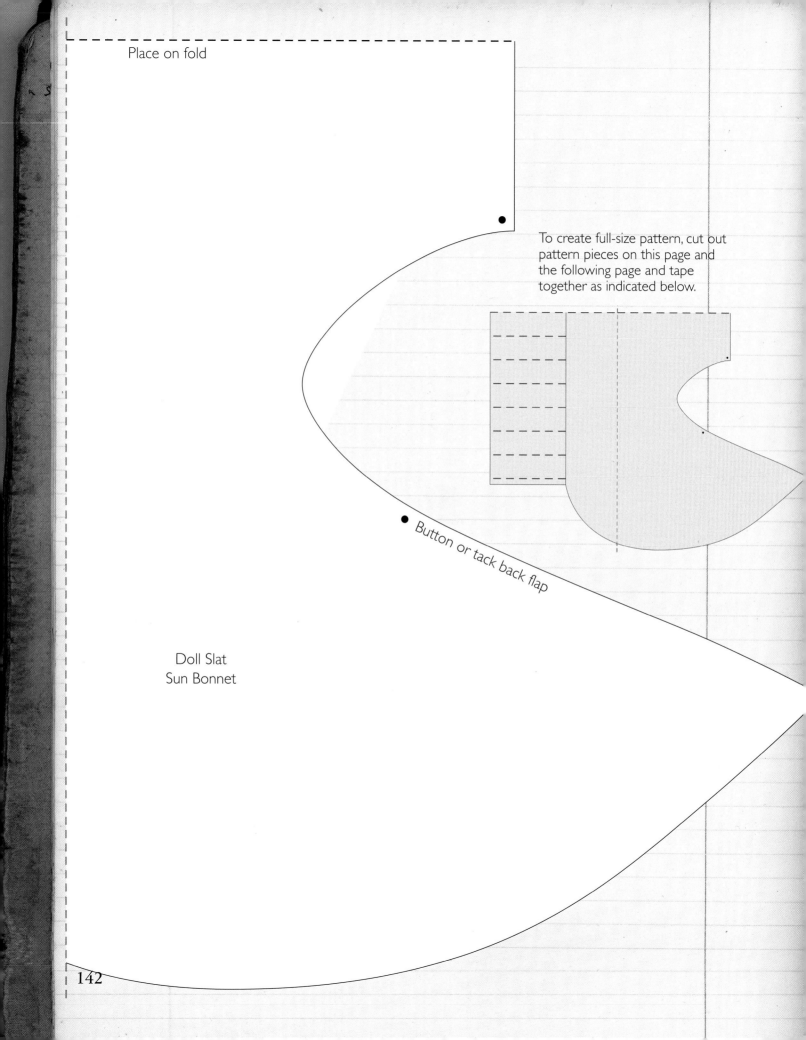

Place on fold

To create full-size pattern, cut out
pattern pieces on this page and
the following page and tape
together as indicated below.

Button or tack back flap

Doll Slat
Sun Bonnet

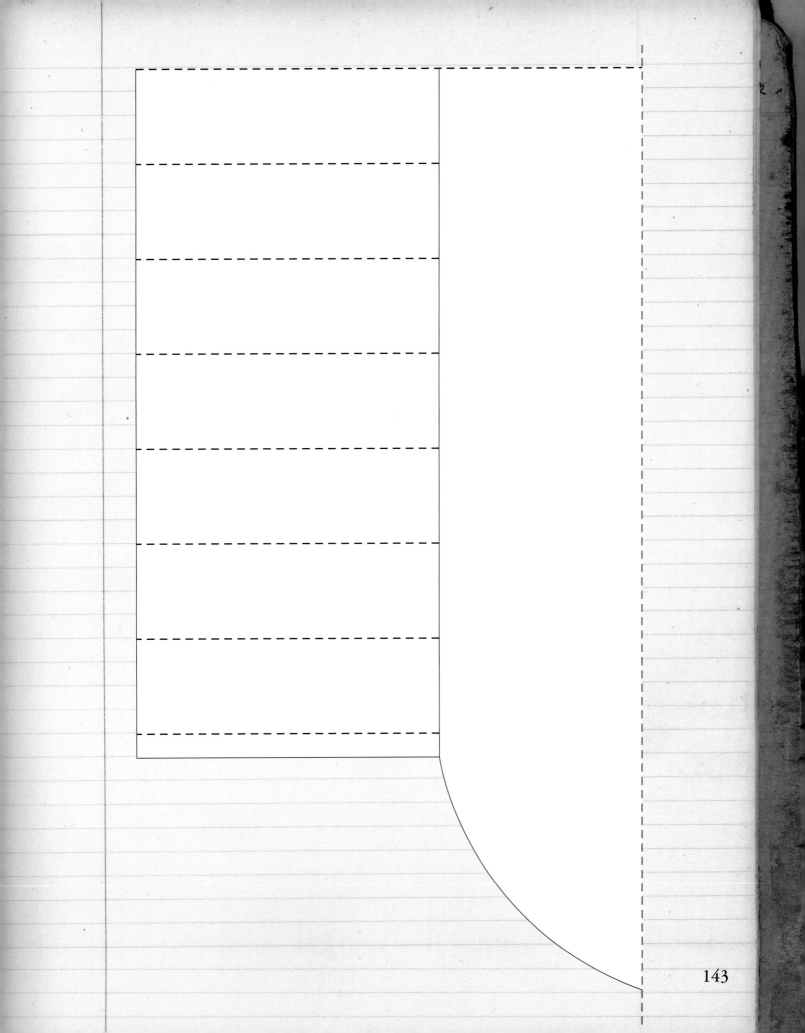

Good Advice & Instructions

146

Good Advice
Instructions for completing
Four Block Quilts

Fabric selection: 100% cotton fabric is, without exception, the best fabric for appliqué. Some wonderful quilts that have passed down through generations of families have come to us in exceptionally good condition. While some families saved the appliqué quilt for special occasions, many have been used, loved and washed — and cotton has proven itself to be very durable.

Fabric preparation: Always test for colorfastness, especially with red fabric. To do this: wet a cotton swab with warm water and place on fabric. Watch for a few minutes to see if any color bleeds onto swab. If it does, wash and rinse fabric until it rinses clear. Wash like colors together. Prewash all fabrics on a short prewash cycle. Dry — remove immediately to avoid wrinkles.

Tools needed:

- Sharp fabric scissors and scissors to cut template plastic and freezer paper.
- #7 or #6 quilting needles for running stitch and straw needles for blind stitch.
- 100% mercerized cotton thread to match colors of your appliqué piece.
- Freezer paper or template plastic.
- Long quilters pins.
- Less desirable thread (such as polyester) can be used for basting.
- Thimble to fit middle finger on sewing hand.
- Clear plastic bags to store appliqué pieces.
- Pincushion and sewing basket to keep project organized.
- #2 lead pencil and white chalk pencil for drawing on dark fabric.
- Yardstick.
- Clover bias maker: one-half inch and one inch size.

Techniques:

- Draw all pattern pieces onto template plastic or freezer paper.
- Beginning with one color, cut out 2-4 appliqués at a time. You will have to trace the template over each appliqué to get a pencil guideline. To keep order, when all pieces of one color have been cut out, stack these pieces and run a knotted thread through them all OR place all the pieces together in a plastic bag. Read specific directions first.
- Prepare the background of each block for placement of pieces by folding the block in half, pressing gently, then in half again, pressing again. Then fold the block diagonally twice and press gently. See General Directions with Coxcomb & Currant for illustrations of this. Be careful not to stretch the block.
- Stems and vines that are curved should be cut on the bias.
- Flowers that have several layers should be sewn together as a unit, then appliquéd in place on the background block.
- Keep several needles threaded so you may continue to appliqué at a brisk pace without losing your rhythm.

Prepare your appliqué pieces

- **Baste.** If you are a beginner, baste all the pieces under ¼" seams before appliquéing in place. Also, baste appliqués in their correct positions, overlapping when necessary. It is not necessary to baste under an edge that will be under another piece.
- **Hand appliqué with freezer paper on top.** Using freezer paper on the right side of the appliqué is a great guide for turning under the edge consistently. As you are needle-turning, guide the seam allowance to just even with the edge of the freezer paper. After all is sewn, remove paper and you are finished. No cutting behind the appliqué to remove the paper is necessary.

Choose the technique that best fits your skill and appliqué experience.

Appliqué techniques

Top running stitch appliqué

- Many antique quilts were sewn with a running stitch to secure the appliqué. This basic hand-sewing stitch, the one we use for quilting and piecing, is the easiest hand appliqué stitch. I recommend this technique for beginning appliqué artists because the stitches can be easily seen on the top of the appliqué. The stitch is speedy and you may take three to four stitches at a time. Although this technique flattens the appliqué somewhat, it is secure and gives a finished look. A different colored thread can add a little color or a strong outline to your appliqué.

- Prepare the appliqué by placing the pattern on the top side of the fabric. Trace around the appliqué with a #2 lead pencil. If the fabric is dark, use a chalk pencil. This line is the guideline for turning under the ¼" seam allowance.
- Cut, adding ¼" seam allowance around the pencil line.
- I recommend that beginners pre-baste each appliqué piece by turning under the ¼" seam on the pencil line and basting the edges over. Baste all appliqué patches to the background, tucking under points and raw edges.
- Stitch, gathering your fabric up on your needle as you go, about 1/16 – 1/8" from the edge of the appliquéd piece. You don't want to do a stab stitch (one stitch at a time).
- Use contrasting thread to show your even stitches.

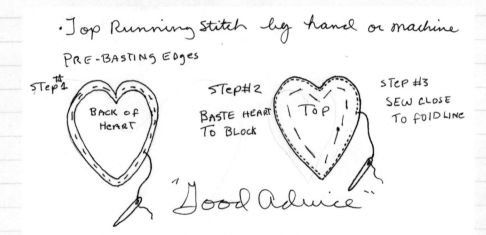

Blind stitch

- Pin and baste each layer of the design in place. Knot a thread and bring your needle from the wrong side of the background block and through the folded edge of the appliqué. Take

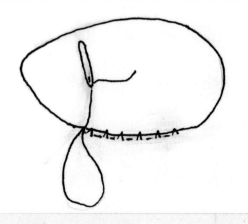

needle back down thru block and back up again about 1/16" from the last stitch into the fold of the appliqué. Use your needle to turn under the raw edge, press with your finger and hold in place with your thumb. I move my thumb and finger press about 1" ahead of my last stitch. (Finger press 1/2" ahead of the last stitch, using needle to turn under raw edge of appliqué.) This technique gives a rounded "lifted" edge to the appliqué.

Turning Points

For turning leaf points or sharp flower spikes, use an envelope turn by folding down the tip first, then folding both sides of leaf over the leaf tip. If the leaf or flower is wide, just stitch to 1/4" of the point, pivot and fold under the other edge and continue sewing.

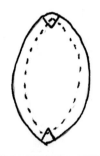

- Fold in tips of leaves first, then fold in seam on all sides of leaf before you appliqué around the tip of the leaf.
- Take a whipstitch or two over the tip of leaf to secure it.
- The closer the stitches are (1/16"), the more rounded the appliqué becomes. Take firm stitches (give a tug on each one, but be careful not to pinch fabric), as appliqué tends to relax. Begin and end with a knot on the back of the block.

Needle-fanning

When a block has deep curves to sew: As you sew to the concave (inner) curve, stop stitching 1/4" from the beginning of the curve. Turn to the next curve and fan the needle, turning the needle from left to right as you take a stitch, ending back to the right to pull edge under firmly, catching all threads back under the seam allowance.

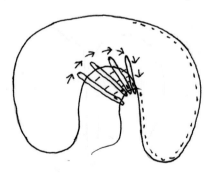

The seam directly under the curve will be narrow, but several fannings will secure stray threads. Hold turned under seam all firmly with thumb and continue to sew into the curve. Take two or three extra close whip-stitches as you round the curve.

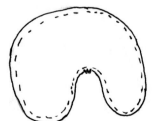

Step by step machine appliqué

Machine appliqué that looks like hand appliqué

- Prewash and dry fabric. This makes freezer paper adhere better. Adjust pattern to adapt to machine appliqué by rounding off sharp points and corners.

- Trace pattern pieces onto freezer paper. If the pattern is not symmetrical draw on the shiny side of freezer paper. If design is symmetrical, draw on the dull side of freezer paper. To cut several patterns at a time, layer three sheets of freezer paper on ironing board. With the tip of the iron, press small "points" in the designs to fuse the three layers together. Cut out all pattern pieces drawn on freezer paper, cutting on the pencil line.

- Work with one color at a time. Lay fabric on ironing board, right side down (wrong side of fabric facing up).

- Set iron on cotton/linen setting so it's hot. I use a steam setting.

- Lay out pattern pieces, at least 1/2" apart, shiny side down on fabric.

- Iron on each piece, making sure each has room to cut a 1/4" seam allowance. Iron the patterns two times for good adherence. Let fabric cool before moving it, and handle gently so freezer paper doesn't lift off. The paper may be re-ironed or lifted and placed in another position if necessary.

- Cut out, adding 1/4" seam allowance around the pattern piece. Re-iron if freezer paper comes loose.

- The most important step in this process is gluing the 1/4" seam allowance over the edge of the freezer paper pattern. If the edges are not smoothly turned, the appliqué looks rough and unattractive. Practice to perfect a smooth edge. Tuck fabric into corners and press the tips of leaves to a nice point. Anyone may achieve these skills with patience and practice. This preparation takes longer, but the sewing time is unbelievably fast and results in a very smooth professional look.

I use a glue stick that is friendly to fabrics, acid-free and washable. A plastic placemat serves as a nice portable work surface. Have a damp washcloth handy to wipe sticky fingers.

- The next most important step is to match the color of thread to the color of the appliqué. I use a machine embroidery cotton thread - 50 weight - to sew the appliqué. Do not use plastic filament to sew: only cotton next to cotton. Also, do not use polyester thread, even if it is cotton covered. The plastic eventually breaks and the poly is too strong and cuts into the cotton. Use the same thread for the top and bobbin thread.

- Two stitches work well for machine appliqué. The first is a **top running stitch**, set on a medium stitch length. Experiment with the stitch length you like best. Simply stitch just inside the folded edge of the appliqué and sew a straight line. Many 19th century quiltmakers appliquéd their quilts on their treadle sewing machines.

- The **blind stitch** looks as if you hand-appliquéd. Set your machine to the blind or hem stitch setting, then dial the stitch length to a very short length: between 0 and 1. Run the edge of the needle right next to the edge of the appliqué. The machine will take two stitches into the background and one v-shaped stitch into the edge of the appliqué.

- Practice with patterns until you feel the confidence to start on your quilt. Believe it or not, the faster you run the machine, the more control you have over the accuracy of the stitching.

Follow the directions for lay-out of the pattern pieces with each pattern. Sew all appliqué.

To remove the freezer paper, follow these steps:

- Turn block to back side and use blunt tip scissors to cut out back. Be very careful in this procedure. Cut 1/4" away from stitch line on back of each appliqué. I have cut little holes where they were not planned by going too fast and not keeping the block flat as I worked.

- Next, place the block in the washer and let it soak in warm water for ten minutes. This will loosen the glue and make the paper easier to remove. Spin dry.

- While still damp, stretch the block by giving a gentle "snap" or jerk on the bias between opposite corners. This will loosen the freezer paper for easy removal. Remember, the close stitching has already perforated the paper.
- Press block while still damp, blocking it back to its original shape.

Cordless flat piping

19th century dressmakers reinforced the seams of their dresses with a corded piping. This practice sometimes was used in quiltmaking as a decorative touch. Usually sewn between the blocks, it brings a bit of color and definition to the edges of blocks and binding. I like to use a contrasting color such as red for the Sunflower quilt.

To make cordless flat piping:

- Rotary cut one-inch strips on the cross-grain (not the bias) from fold to selvedge.

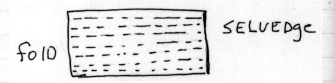

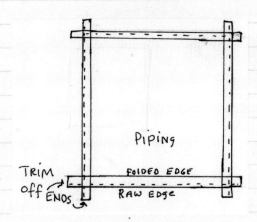

- Fold strips in half and press, wrong sides together.
- Place strip inside block edge—raw edge to raw edge—as you would binding. Let strips extend off edge of block. Sew strip to block with a ¼" seam allowance.

Making bias strips

After years of struggling with border vines for my appliqué patterns, I invented a tool for marking the borders first with shallow, medium or deep curves. The Vine Line® is a handy tool and may be found at your favorite quilt shop.

Another great tool for making bias strips is the Clover® bias maker. Strips made with it can be laid over the Vine Line markings for smooth, curvy vines.

How to make bias with the bias maker:

- Cut one-inch fabric strips on the bias for ½" finished bias strips or two-inch strips for 1" finished bias. For the width of your desired bias strip, double the finished size of the maker.
- Cut a V into the end of the bias strip and go to the ironing board. Lay out the long strip on the board. Push the V thru the large end

153

of the bias maker. Gently pull the handle and hold the iron on the end of the strip. As you slowly pull the maker along the strip, followed with the iron, the seam allowances are turned in and pressed evenly. Gently wrap finished bias strips over a cardboard roll to keep the folds in place until you are ready to place the strip on your marked border.

Borders

- Generally borders on antique quilts are squared—not mitered. The top and bottom border are appliquéd first and then sewn to the four blocks. Then, the appliquéd side borders are sewn to the sides of the four blocks. If there are multiple borders, repeat in the same order.

- For corner designs, pin borders to the appliquéd top and mark the placement of the corner appliqués. Then the rest of the border appliqués can be placed to correctly "meet" the corner appliqués.

- For wandering vines, either place by "eye" or use the small, medium, or deep curve templates for placement of vine on the border.

- Vines may loop around the corners or meander off each end of the border.

- Remember, you may add berries, leaves or other designs to cover swags or vines that do not quite meet or overlap. This adds more interest and charm to these folk quilts. Feel free to design the border as you wish. Our great-grandmothers did not always concern themselves with matching the borders and the blocks. They put tulip borders around rose or coxcomb blocks, drew leaf patterns that do not resemble anything in the natural world, combined birds and animals with swags and tassels. Many borders were simple vines with a rosette and leaf as the only design element. Others are filled with dozens of motifs that probably took as much time to appliqué as the set blocks. Mix the designs with images that do not go together and have some fun with your borders.

Machine appliquéd stems and vines

Cut bias strips 1½" wide for narrow stems, or 2" wide for a heavier vine.

- Fold strip in half, raw edges even.
- Pin folded strip in place, pinning curves to hold them in place.
- Machine stitch ¼" from raw edge of strip.
- Fold over folded edge of strip and appliqué in place, over raw edge of strip.
- If other stems connect with the vine, lay them in place and fold over as you stitch down the vine.

Making berries and currants

To make berries and currants (or any round shape), use sticky removable labels found at office supply stores for large, medium and small circles. Place sticky labels on fabric, cut ¼" seam allowance and glue or hand baste the edges under. Remove labels and appliqué.

Dog tooth borders and edges

To make dogtooth borders, cut strips of fabric 3" wide (or desired size) and the desired length. Measure and mark 2" intervals. Measure your strips to your borders and figure the math from corner to corner or follow these instructions for a less formal look.

Mark every two inches and make a 1" cut (deeper if borders are wider). Baste strip to bottom edge of each border.

Fold points over ¼" and sides to create pyramids. Baste and appliqué these points to create a dogtooth edge. You may pin each tooth as you go, or pre-baste, but you will soon be able to just finger press as you sew. If the points are deep, I overlap the sides of pyramids to create a tight corner that is easier to sew.

Sometimes corners will not always come out exactly. That is part of the charm of 19th century quilts. However, you may appliqué an extra "dogtooth" triangle over the corners to make them look more even.

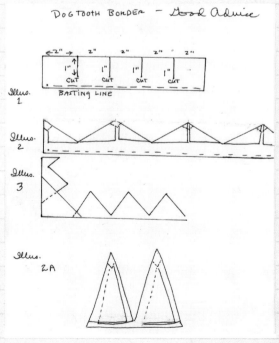

155

Quilting and finishing advice

- Designs for quilting were traded and shared by our foremothers. Most quilting designs were traced from old quilts, created by women long before printed patterns were available.

- Four-, six- or nine-block appliqué quilts can create unusual space that calls for elongated quilt designs. Background filler designs do a beautiful job of filling in spaces that do not accommodate conventional quilt designs.

- Many 19th century appliqué quilts were quilted with straight double or triple lines one-eighth-inch apart, running diagonally over the entire surface of the top. The lines marched right over the appliqué work, ignoring the designs that we would quilt around today.

This method protected the appliqué pieces—the first to wear out from use. Of course, the straight-line quilting could also be done more quickly than fancy plumes and circular designs.

- Trace the quilt patterns on to your quilt top by placing the top over the printed pattern, then lightly draw over the lines or make small dots. If the pattern lines are too light to show through the quilt fabric, darken the patterns with a black marker. Tops may also be marked from the top with commercial plastic templates. Straight lines and grids may be marked with a yardstick. Use a #2 lead pencil. It will usually fade away as you quilt or with the first or second washing, if lines are not too dark. If your fabric is dark, you can create a light table by using a storm window propped between two chairs with a lamp underneath to illuminate the design. Trace, using a white lead dressmaker's pencil or art pencil.

Quilting: Place backing (wrong side up, batting and quilt top (right side up), on a flat surface. Pin and baste all three layers together, smoothing wrinkles. Arrange quilt in hoop. Start in center, working toward the edge, using a single thread and knot, bringing needle through all three layers from underneath side of quilt. Pop the knot through the back layer, thereby securing the knot in the batting layer. Now you are ready to quilt. With the needle at a 45-degree angle, take small running stitches, catching all three layers. To finish off, run the needle under the top layer of the quilt the length of the needle, then trim off the extra thread.

Binding: Cut a two-inch bias strip. Sew end-to-end creating your binding length. Fold binding in half and sew raw edges to the front of the quilt by machine or by hand, either mitering or easing around corners. Turn folded edge of binding to the back of the quilt and appliqué in place, covering the raw edge of the quilt. I use longer blind stitches to sew binding and it goes quicker. There is no need for 1/16" stitches on the binding.

Reverse appliqué

- Reverse appliqué gives a different perception to an appliquéd quilt. Instead of seeing layers of applied patterns standing away from the quilt background, the eye looks into layers of cloth cut down into the "inside" of a quilt design. This gives the design depth and added interest.
- Layer two or more fabrics, pin and baste in place. Cut design from the top fabric, revealing the second fabric beneath. Do not skimp on this underneath piece.
- Turn under 1/4" and appliqué the top layer of cloth to the second layer beneath.

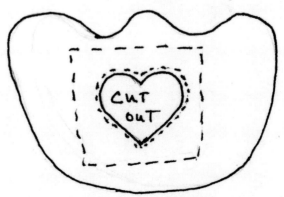

Coxcomb and Currant

"Why yes, why not?"
Size: 92" x 92"

My mother, Esther Richardson, appliquéd her first quilt at the age of 79.
Mother traveled with me on teaching trips to Texas and western Kansas. Having
no real interest in quiltmaking, she often took her golf clubs and played the local
courses while I taught my Appliqué by the Yard classes to quilt guilds.

After hearing several of my lectures about the virtues of four block quilts, she said, "I can't take it anymore. I'm going to make one." Being the practical perfectionist, Mother made a smaller appliqué block to practice her appliqué stitch, then chose this Coxcomb and Currant pattern for her queen-size bed quilt. We shopped for fabrics and she settled on the colors she wanted for her guest room bed. She chose soft green and apricot with a black accent. When I asked her why she chose black, she said "Why yes, why not?"

Here is her quilt. After 18 months of appliqué work, Mother finished her top. My sister Kim, Mother and I marked the top with the clamshell background filler, a one-inch grid, feathers and flower designs using plastic templates. Ann Thomas hand-quilted it in three months.

Yardage, step-by-step general directions and directions specific for this quilt follow.

Yardage for blocks and borders:

Apricot: 2 1/2 yards
- 4 center rosettes B
- 16 large coxcombs E
- 24 buds K in borders

Rust: 1/2 yard
- 16 middle coxcombs D
- 4 small rosettes A

Black: 1/2 yard
- 60 berries H
- 24 1 ½" x 2 ½" rectangles for reverse appliqué on buds in borders

Green: 3 yards
- 24 calyx I for borders
- 16 ferns G
- 25 swags J
- 16 stems F

Background blocks and borders: 6½ yards
- (4) 36 1/2" square
- 10" borders

General Directions—Coxcomb and Currant

Read through all directions before beginning

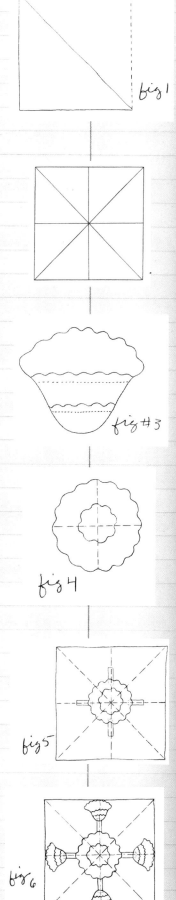

- We are using a coxcomb pattern as an example.
  Add ¼" seam allowance as you cut out the appliqués.
- To begin, prepare the background block by cutting a 36 ½"
square. Measure yardage 36 ½" and fold into a triangle. Remember,
fabric is 40-45" wide so you need to cut approximately 4-9" off to get a
36 ½" square. If you forget the ½" don't worry, your pieces will fit a
35" square, everything can be adjusted to fit. That's one of the virtues
of appliqué!

    See figure 1. Refer to fabric layout guide.

- Fold square in half, then in half again.
- Press on folded lines. Then fold folded square on the diagonal
  and press diagonal lines. These folded/pressed lines serve as a
  placement guide for the appliqués. See figure 2.
- To prepare appliqués, cut a template of each appliqué. You may
  stack your fabric and cut several layers at once, but you will
  need to draw around the template on each piece to give you a
  pencil "turn under" line.
- Draw around templates on the right side of the fabric – cut
  out ¼" from pencil line as no seam allowance has been
  added to the patterns. Cut one color at a time and allow
  plenty of table room, as these blocks are BIG.
- Historically all appliqués are laid out on the background block,
  pinned and basted in place, using the pressed lines as a guide.
  Before this step is taken, however, appliqué the flower or
  center rosette units together before placing them on the block.
  It is much easier to sew smaller units together separately than
  on the 36" block. See figure 3 and 4.
- Now lay out all prepared appliqués, following the pressed lines
  as a guide. Beginning in the center, pin and baste ⅛" from the
  raw edge, remove pins and appliqué in place, tucking
  under the ends of stems and leaves a "good" ¼" – ½"
  under so raw edges do not appear as you sew. See
  figures 5, 6 and 7.

160

- Now the sewing part. I strongly suggest that beginners appliqué in the top running stitch, even pre-basting the appliqués before pinning and basting to the block. This just means that all raw edges of the appliqués are turned under on the pencil line ¼" and basted. This prepares the edges ahead of appliquéing. Yes, it is an extra step, but the beginner has greater success and will love to appliqué. Of course as one improves this step may be eliminated, however, I still pre-baste if several units are to be layered.

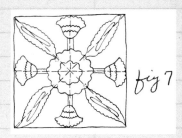

fig 7

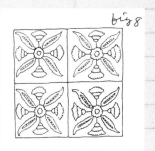

fig 8

- Intermediate and advanced appliquérs may use the blind stitch or machine appliqué using freezer paper techniques. Consult your local quilt shop or quilt guild for appliqué classes, learn all the techniques, then choose what is best for you. In taking a class, you will learn so much more about appliqué techniques, and you will be supporting your shop or guild at the same time.

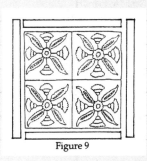

Figure 9

- Do not cut out behind appliqués, as the appliqués need the support of the background block. (You will have to cut the backs out when using the freezer paper technique to remove the paper.)
- Set finished blocks. See figure 8.
- Borders: I do not miter borders. I sew the top and bottom first, then the sides. See figure 9.

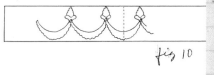

fig 10

- Find the center of the border and swag. Center swag at center of border, then everything is laid out from center. See figure 10.
- Appliqué borders separately from blocks, then sew to body of quilt placing corner swags to meet the two connecting borders. See figure 11.
- Remove all basting.
- To quilt, use background filler patterns for the empty spaces between blocks, such as clamshell, double lines, feathers or diamonds.

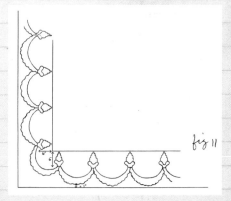

fig 11

Any design will look terrific on these quilts.

- Bind edges. (I like to make a bias binding.) Attach a sleeve. Sign and date your quilt, and you are finished.

Coxcomb & Currant directions

- Follow General Directions above for preparation of background block and appliqué pieces.
- Appliqué small rosette A to large center flower B.
- Appliqué calyx C to middle coxcomb D to top coxcomb E.
- Match center of large rosette A-B to center of background block. Pin in place.
- Pin stem F on horizontal and vertical lines. Pin coxcomb units on horizontal and vertical lines, covering the raw edge of stem.
- To reverse appliqué centers of ferns, cut a slit down the center of each fern on the dotted line shown on the pattern piece. Cut fabric for the insert approximately 3" x 11 ½". (The shape has been outlined on the pattern piece.) DO NOT skimp on this insert piece as you want all raw edges of the slash to disappear onto the insert, and not come up short. Sew insert before basting to block. Appliqué berries H to insert. You may have the background show instead of adding an insert as shown in the quilt.
- Pin ferns G on the diagonal lines, referring to the photo for placement.
- Baste all pieces in place.
- Remove pins and appliqué.
- Sew the blocks together.
- Quilt and bind.

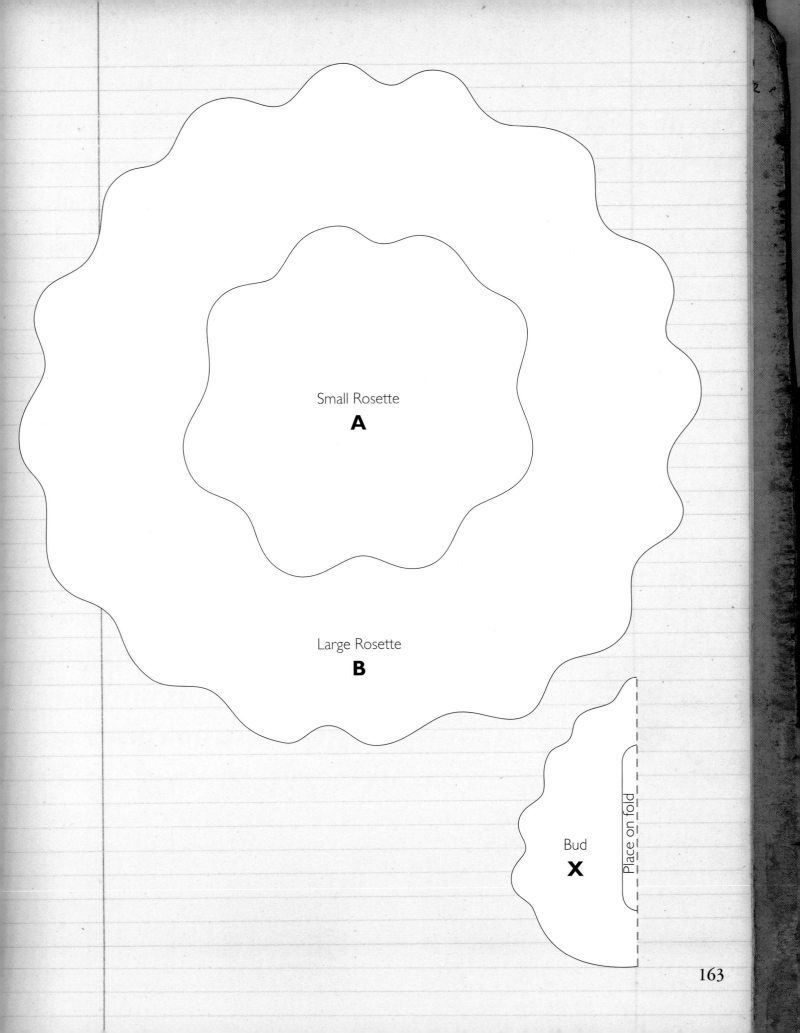

Small Rosette

A

Large Rosette

B

Bud

X

Place on fold

163

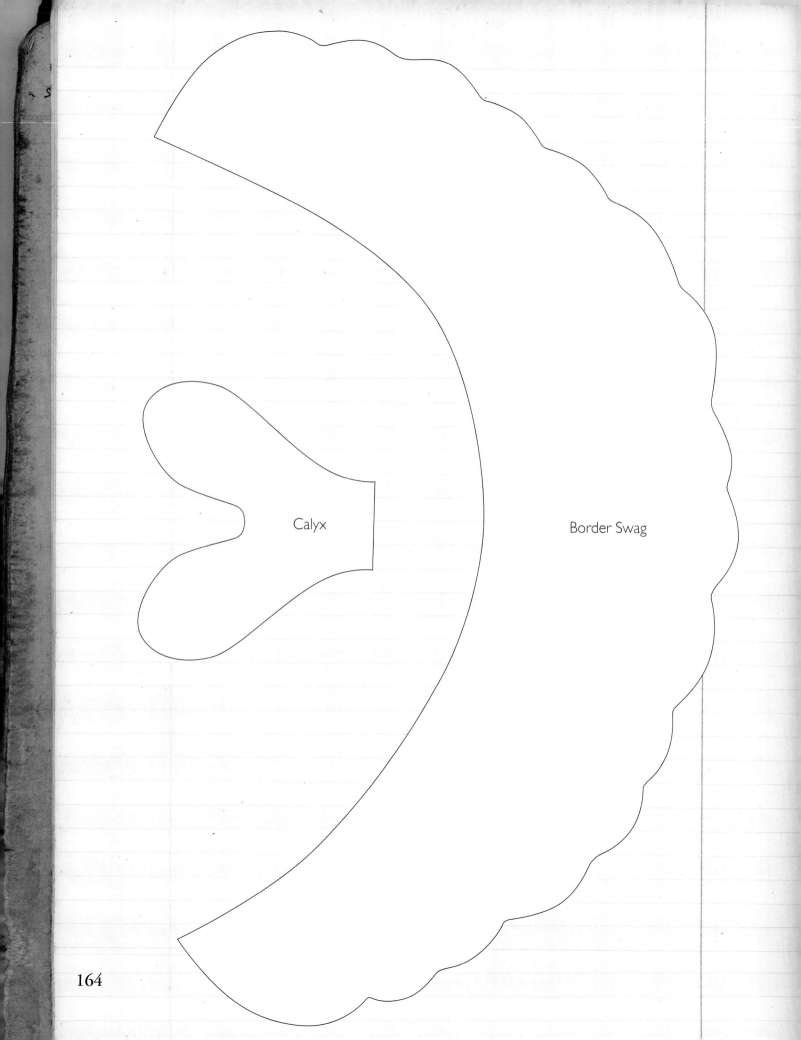

Calyx

Border Swag

164

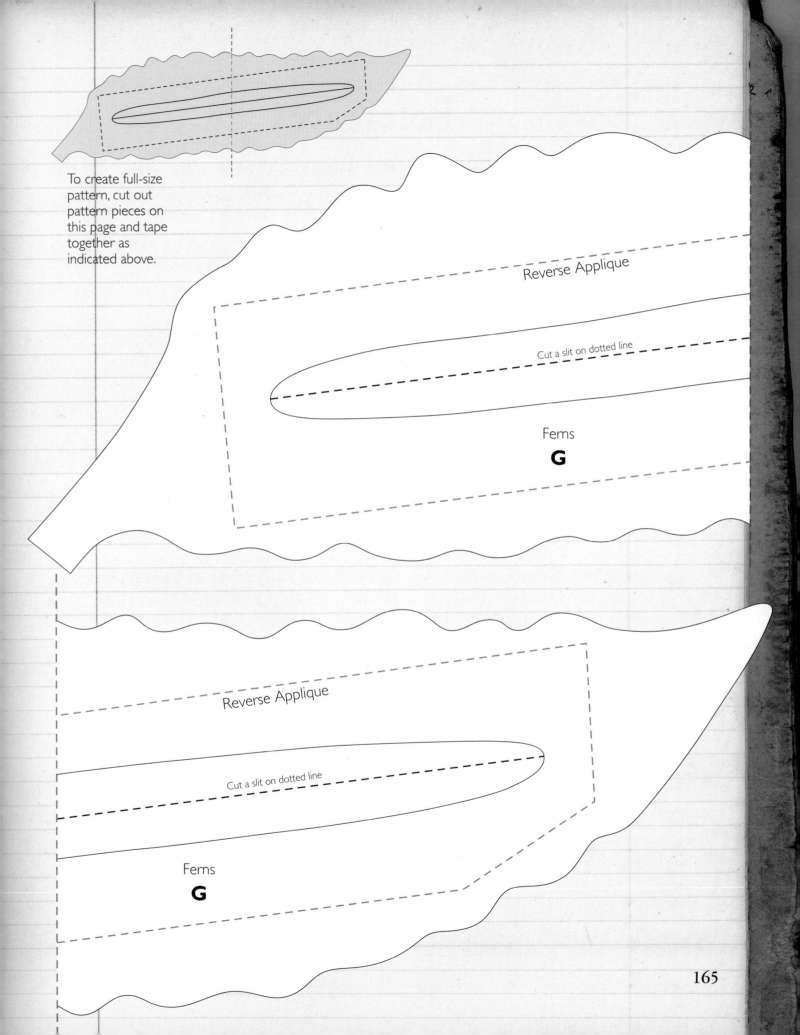

To create full-size pattern, cut out pattern pieces on this page and tape together as indicated above.

Reverse Applique

Cut a slit on dotted line

Ferns

G

Reverse Applique

Cut a slit on dotted line

Ferns

G

References

H. Arnold Barton in Letters From The Promised Land: Swedes in America, 1840-1914 1975, University of Minnesota Press, Minneapolis, Minnesota for the Swedish Pioneer Historical Society.

Mildred Cass Beason in Pioneer Reminiscences (Gove County [Kansas] Historical Association, 1985).

Philip L. Gerber, ed., in Bachelor Bess, The Homesteading Letters of Elizabeth Corey, 1909-1919, Foreword by Paul Corey, Afterword by Wayne Franklin, 1990, University of Iowa Press, Iowa City, Iowa.

Grace Snyder and Nellie Snyder Yost, "No Time on My Hands" 1986, University of Nebraska Press, Lincoln, Nebraska.

Joanna Stratton in Pioneer Women: Voices from the Kansas Frontier (Simon & Schuster: New York, 1981).

L. William Travis in Pioneering in Kansas: Iowa to Kansas in an Ox Wagon. Experiences of Capt. Charles M. Sears and Family in the '50s. Pamphlet, Kansas State Historical Society.

Recommended sources

Karla Menaugh and Cherie Ralston in Quiltmaker's Guide to Fine Machine Appliqué, 2002, Sunflower Pattern Co-operative. Crystal-clear descriptions of this modern technique.

More Kansas City Star Quilt Books

You can find these other great Kansas City Star Quilt books at www.PickleDish.com:

Star Quilts I : One Piece At A Time

Star Quilts II : More Kansas City Star Quilts

Star Quilts III : Outside the Box

Star Quilts IV : Prairie Flower: A Year On The Plains

Star Quilts V : The Sister Blocks

Star Quilts VI : Kansas City Quiltmakers

Star Quilts VII : O'Glory: American Quilt Blocks from The Kansas City Star

Star Quilts VIII : Hearts & Flowers: Hand Applique From Start to Finish

Star Quilts IX : Roads & Curves Ahead

Star Quilts X : Celebration of American Life: Applique Patterns Honoring a Nation and Its People

Star Quilts XI : Women of Grace & Charm: A Quilting Tribute to the Women Who Served in World War II

Star Quilts XII : A Heartland Album: More Techniques in Hand Applique

Star Quilts XIII : Quilting A Poem: Designs Inspired by America's Poets

Star Quilts XIV : Carolyn's Paper-Pieced Garden: Patterns for Miniature and Full-Sized Quilts

Star Quilts XV : Murders On Elderberry Road: Mystery Book

Star Quilts XVI : Friendships in Bloom: Round Robin Quilts

Star Quilts XVII : Baskets of Treasures: Designs Inspired by Life Along the River

Star Quilts XVIII: Heart & Home: Unique American Women and the Houses that Inspire

Project books:

Santa's Parade of Nursery Rhymes

Fan Quilt Memories: A Selection of Fan Quilts from The Kansas City Star